CANADA

CANADA

I PEYTO LAKE, ALBERTA

CANADA

PHOTOGRAPHED BY

PETER VARLEY

INTRODUCTION BY KILDARE DOBBS

176 PHOTOGRAVURE PLATES

8 PLATES IN COLOUR

TORONTO

MACMILLAN OF CANADA

TEXT PRINTED IN GREAT BRITAIN BY JARROLD AND SONS LTD NORWICH
GRAVURE PRINTED BY D. H. GREAVES LTD SCARBOROUGH

I

MEN AND NATIONS live by imagination, by the dreams that relate them to their land and its past. It is in these myths that one looks, cautiously, for national character. The myth of the Frontier, for example. There actually was – and there still is – a Frontier in Canada. Prospectors, trappers, and lumberjacks still brawl in the boom-town honky-tonks and beer-parlours. Mounties still occasionally hitch up a dog-team to go out and get their man on the frozen tundra. I have talked to Beaver Indians in their teepees by the Halfway River in northern British Columbia: they actually did wear beaded moccasins and speak like the redskins in television serials. To this extent myth may accord with fact.

Yet the myth may be misleading. The prospector, more scientist than rough-neck, is not what he was: 'The day of the jackass leading the jackass is gone', as one of them told me. And the trapper – the trapper is vanishing, ruined by competition from the fur-farms. The lumberjack has abandoned his axe for a buzz-saw and turns out to be a family man and a church-goer. As for the Mountie, he may well be a youth with pimples, interested in dogs only if their owners have failed to license them. And the Beaver Indians, wearing galoshes over their moccasins, are listening to rock-'n'-roll on transistor radios. Finally, all these people and the Frontier itself are as remote from the experience of most ordinary Canadians as they are from the experience of a bank-clerk in the Bronx or a Stevenage typist. Does this destroy the myth? Not at all.

For in the secret places of his imagination every Canadian sawing firewood at his summer cottage is a lumberjack, every suburbanite on skis a *coureur de bois*, every Sunday canoer a *voyageur*. The myth (as beer advertisers well understand) even influences his drinking. He attacks each beer as if it were his first after months of abstinence in the bush.

The myth of the Frontier is, of course, shared with other North Americans, like the myths of triumphant free enterprise and of the West. There are also more definitive myths which are uniquely Canadian: myths of the United Empire Loyalists, of the conquered but undefeated

French Canadians, of the 'true North strong and free'. To call them myths is not to deny their truth. Some of them are rooted in the facts of history and geography.

Canada is the biggest small nation in the world. Surpassed in size only by the U.S.S.R. and China, it covers almost four million square miles of the earth's surface. Of this immense territory a mere half-million square miles is effectively occupied, and ninety per cent of its comparatively small population of nineteen million is huddled in a narrow band of settlements within two hundred miles of the United States border. Nor is this small nation uniform in language and culture. Some three and a half million Canadians, mostly in the province of Quebec, speak French only. About twelve and a half million speak only English. And though a further two and a half million (again, mostly in Quebec) speak both languages, there are a quarter of a million Canadians who speak neither. Other significant minorities speak German, Italian, Ukrainian, Chinese, Japanese, Hungarian – and in Cape Breton, Nova Scotia, there are some hundreds of descendants of immigrant Scottish Highlanders whose mother-tongue is still Gaelic.

This plural society exists in the shadow of the richest and most powerful nation in the history of the world. Its ten self-governing provinces are ranged in Indian file along the northern border of the United States for a distance of almost 4,000 miles. Nova Scotia, New Brunswick, Quebec, Ontario, Manitoba, Saskatchewan, Alberta, British Columbia: they follow one another, east to west, like so many stops on the transcontinental railway which made Confederation possible. Ferries join Newfoundland, a latecomer to Confederation (1949), and Prince Edward Island to the railway system. Each region is a northward extension of a similar one in the United States: the Maritime or Atlantic provinces are part of the New England Appalachians; Quebec and Ontario are on the lower and upper reaches of the St Lawrence River system; the Prairie provinces are part of the great plains; British Columbia, almost entirely mountainous, is a segment of the continent's high rocky spine, the cordillera that runs along the Pacific from Alaska to Mexico.

The railway (or rather two railways, the privately owned Canadian Pacific and the State's Canadian National) is a straight line ruled from ocean to ocean against the grain of continental geography by the chief engineer of Confederation, Canada's first Prime Minister, Sir John A. Macdonald. 'The railway line, that tenuous thread which bound Canada to both the great oceans and made her a nation, lay with one end in the darkness of Nova Scotia and the other in a British Columbia noon.' The thought occurs with the force of inspiration to a character in one of the novels of Hugh MacLennan, an eloquent writer on national themes. Perhaps no one but a Canadian could think of a railway in just that way. More – perhaps no one but a Canadian who has deliberately cultivated a national consciousness.

II CAPE SPEAR, NEWFOUNDLAND

Travelling on the transcontinental passenger trains, one is reminded that the great age of railways that devised Confederation has gone for ever. Most travellers, businessmen or vacationers in a hurry, prefer to cross Canada by jet airliner. The trains are half empty. Powerful Diesel locomotives have displaced steam, but the coaches retain the comfort of an earlier age. White-jacketed Negro porters, the starched linen and gleaming silver of dining-cars, the curiously Victorian uniforms of conductors and other officials are pleasantly evocative of the nineteenth century. The Canada viewed in a gentlemanly way from dome-cars or the windows of luxurious 'drawing-rooms' (significant archaism) is all Sir John Macdonald's.

This Canada of the railway is only a fraction of the whole country. There is also the older Canada of the waterways. The vast river-system of the St Lawrence and the Great Lakes carried seventeenth-century explorers, fur-traders, and missionaries of New France deep into the continent. They and their rivals and successors of the fur-trading companies – the Hudson's Bay, XY, and North West companies – were to cast a web of forts and trading-posts over the whole land, a fur empire with headquarters in Montreal, its birchbark canoes and flat-bottomed York boats plying the myriad lakes and rivers of the Canadian Shield.

The Shield is an immense geophysical feature peculiar to Canada. Its nearly two million square miles of hard pre-Cambrian rock coils round Hudson Bay, crossing the north of all the provinces from Newfoundland to Saskatchewan. In its southern reaches, which cover most of Ontario and Quebec, it is a country of forests, lakes, rivers, and rocky outcrops, a beautiful, implacable wilderness. It is utterly intractable to cultivation.

By the turn of the eighteenth and nineteenth centuries the trader-explorers Alexander Mackenzie and Simon Fraser had crossed the continental divide and struggled overland to the Pacific. Some notion of the scale of these activities is hinted in a few statistics of Canada's waterways. The St Lawrence system is two thousand miles long. Lake Ontario, smallest of its great lakes, has an area of 7,540 square miles; Lake Superior, the largest (the 'shining big sea water' of Longfellow's *Hiawatha*), 31,820 square miles. The Mackenzie, Canada's longest river, is 2,635 miles from its source to its Arctic estuary; the Yukon is 1,979 miles long, 714 of which are in Canada; the Fraser runs 850 miles to the Pacific.

Some of the waterways are still in use. The St Lawrence system, ice-bound in winter, in summer supports a thriving merchant marine. Since the St Lawrence Seaway opened in 1959, ocean shipping plies between the lake-ports and the great trading-centres of the world.

Newer communications have created new Canadas. The era of the bush pilots opened the North for exploitation of its rich mineral deposits. In the late 1920s and throughout the 1930s these incredible airmen pioneered the techniques of aerial mineralogical exploration. Flying their primitive machines over some of the most savage country in the world, compasses spinning crazily from closeness to the magnetic pole, they were often lost and sometimes killed. Sub-zero temperatures for which their engines had not been designed often forced them to thaw lubricating oil over stoves. Sometimes the oil caught fire. Sometimes the pilots were grounded for days and weeks in the bush, depending on their rifles and luck for survival. Because of what they learned, the two-fifths of Canada that lies outside the provinces is now more or less accessible. The Yukon Territory, the Northwest Territories, even the Arctic archipelago, are effectively bound to Canada.

The newest Canada of the automobile and the super-highway is still in its infancy. The Trans-Canada Highway, all but completed, runs with its connecting ferries all the way from St John's, Newfoundland, to Tofino on the west coast of Vancouver Island. So far its effect, and the effect of other super-highways, has been to increase urban sprawl and hasten rural depopulation. In Central Canada its by-passes have had the more pleasing result of allowing sleepy small towns to relapse, comparatively free of traffic, into their former complacent calm.

II

In theory, all the Canadas meet in Ottawa. In practice the federal capital is merely a political centre, a romantic small city of trees, open space, and cascading water. The Gothic fantasy of Parliament Hill, dominated by its tall Peace Tower, looks over the chasm of the Ottawa River from English-speaking Ontario to the city of Hull in French-speaking Quebec. This Hill, significantly close to the railway station, is the nerve-centre of Confederation: the House of Commons with its British inheritance of mace, Speaker, and majority rule, and its North American 'omnibus' political parties; the rheumaticky Senate; the offices of the Prime Minister and the Leader of the Opposition as well as the great departments of a modern government. At a discreet distance, Rideau Hall, with a heavy air of Public Works, houses the Governor-General, who represents the Crown. Here, in the great gilded throne-room, foreign diplomats from the city's embassies and legations present their credentials. And from here, at the beginning of each session of Parliament, His Excellency (now a Canadian, no longer an imperial proconsul) sets out in all the glitter of vice-regal pomp with cavalry, coach, and plumed head-dress to read the Speech from the Throne in French and English.

The judiciary is present in the Supreme Court of Canada on Wellington Street: nine scarlet-robed justices, one of them the Chief Justice, who form the ultimate tribunal. Their work in hearing appeals is complex, for though there is a single criminal code for the whole

III DORIES IN MAHONE BAY, NEAR BLUE ROCKS, NOVA SCOTIA

country, there is a mass of purely provincial law – notably the civil code of Quebec, which is French in origin. Because appellants have the right to be heard in either official language at least four of the judges are French-speaking.

Ottawa houses other national institutions, fiscal, administrative, and cultural. Probably the most famous is the Royal Canadian Mounted Police. Tourists admire their scarlet tunics and the impeccable horsemanship of their famous musical ride. Reactionary but disciplined, the Mounties enforce the criminal code in eight of the provinces as well as in the Yukon and the Northwest Territories.

Well over a third of Ottawa is directly engaged in government or political work. Like Washington it's a city of civil servants. Responsible, intelligent, and, sometimes, self-important, Ottawans talk political shop interminably.

In winter, its rivers locked in ice, the baronial extravagances of its public buildings stark against snow, Ottawa takes on a Victorian grandeur. Figures in dark topcoats and fur hats come and go with attaché cases, moving with the confident tread of men close to power.

Yet though Sir John Macdonald, in drafting the British North America Act of 1867 which is still the base of Canada's constitution, sought to create a dominant central government, Ottawa's power to hold Confederation together is subject to heavy centrifugal strain. In the 1960s an awakening French Canada is showing discontent with the old railway constitution.

Each province has its own lieutenant-governor, its own elected legislature, premier, and political parties, its own Supreme Court. Autonomous within the subjects of legislation reserved to them by the B.N.A. Act, the provinces are theoretically equal. In practice some are far more powerful than others. Quebec, as the guardian of French-Canadian language and culture, is more than a province. To many *Canadiens*, Quebec is their nation.

More generally, the rich and populous provinces, Ontario and British Columbia no less than Quebec, seek to increase their autonomy. The weaker rely on a strong Ottawa.

III

There is no such town as Friendsville. But I can imagine it, a composite of Canadian dreams of small-town life. For perhaps no North American myth is more pervasive in Canada than this one of the friendly small town.

Approach by car; a sign at the town limits reads: 'WELCOME TO FRIENDS-VILLE. Population 5,323. *Watch Out for Our Children*'. A second sign flashes, as it were, the municipal credentials – the badges of all the service clubs in town: Lions, Kiwanis, Rotarians, Oddfellows, Masons, Moose. Tall elms shade the street which in this part is residential. A few elegant old houses of wood-frame construction, painted white, sit well back from the sidewalk behind unfenced lawns. (To put up fences would be a sign of distrustful reserve.) On their gingerbread porches or verandas elderly ladies in rocking-chairs are knitting socks for charity. They watch fondly over their spectacles while small, freckled boys in tee-shirts and jeans hurry by with fishing-poles and cans of dew worms, heading for the creek. One of the ladies ('the girls' as they call themselves) has just baked a batch of cookies 'as good as store-boughten cookies' – and is now on the alert for children to give them to.

Friendsville people get most of their pleasure from helping other people. As the Reeve puts it, 'Why, I'm just tickled to death to be able to do something for the other fellow.' Take Doc Murray, the general practitioner who lives over there in the pink clapboard ranch-bungalow – the one with the aluminium screen-door ornamented with the letter M. He never neglects a call, he's killing himself with work, yet he's so reluctant to collect bills that he hasn't had a new car for all of three years.

The centre of Friendsville is Main Street. There are several general stores, a hardware, a drugstore, the town 'character'. (Friendsville people are reticent with strangers about the character, but among themselves they enjoy stories of his drunken exploits.) There are two banks and three churches. In the short-order restaurant, run by a grumpy old Chinese with a heart of gold, there's a notice that says: 'Sunday Morning. A Fine Morning to Attend the Church of Your Choice.' A stout, smiling nymphet in a white coat two sizes too small hands the menu: the 'special' today is roast beef sandwich, french fries and cole slaw, home-baked apple pie. 'Will you have your beverage now or later?' she asks.

The myth has it that everyone in Friendsville knows everyone else, helps each other in trouble, is free of all snobbery and class distinction. Admitted that some are richer than others – the undertaker for one (or 'funeral director' as he prefers to be called) is palpably more prosperous than his neighbours – but no one is too grand to sit down to supper in the church basement with the folks. And all the businessmen are working selflessly to attract industry to the town: it just seems wrong to keep such a delightful little place to themselves.

The life of Friendsville is charmingly set forth in Stephen Leacock's *Sunshine Sketches of a Little Town*, a portrait of his own Orillia, Ontario, in which every native Canadian discerns the features of his home town. The French-Canadian equivalent is a little different: here there is only one church, big and gaunt under its tin steeple, and the good-hearted townsmen are obedient, if critical, sons of *Monsieur le Curé*. But the essentials are the same: plain living and neighbourly hearts.

14

IV MONTREAL, QUEBEC

Probably most native Canadians have grown up in towns much like Friendsville. Nor is the myth very misleading. Small-town Canadians are friendly, do help one another, and have managed to achieve something like a classless society. Yet if lawns are unfenced and doors hospitably open, small-town minds tend to be firmly closed. And though Friendsville's social distinctions are based on the comparatively harmless standard of money, they still exist. Because they live close together and know one another so intimately, Friendsville people feel watched and hunted. In defence they sometimes grow hypocritical and secretive.

The myth of Friendsville grew in an age when Canada was predominantly rural and agricultural. That age, like the era of the steam railway that gave birth to Confederation, has already passed into history. Yet the ghost of Friendsville lingers to haunt great metropolitan centres like Montreal, Toronto, and Vancouver, and to bring its warmth and furtiveness to the life of their exploding suburbs.

Roadside sign as you leave Friendsville: 'THANK YOU. COME AGAIN.'

The growth of Canada's great cities has been mainly at the suburban fringe. Though an increasing number of city-dwellers are taking to life in apartment buildings, most, like Friends-villians, prefer to own houses. Though planners and economists insist that the small, detached houses that are spreading over the farmlands like a creeping fungus are aesthetically, socially, and economically undesirable, they seem to be the kind of housing Canadians prefer. They are becoming a nation of property-owners, a fact reflected in the conservatism of their politics.

Suburban life, with its coffee klatsches and neighbourhood parties, becomes a kind of affluent Friendsville. But there is one marked difference. Suburban subdivisions seem to be inhabited by people of a single age-group. If there are children on a street, it's unlikely that there will be any old people. Grandparents are a disappearing breed, at least so far as the young are concerned. The suburban family is being stripped down to its basic unit of father, mother, and children. The grandparents come from city apartments to call on week-ends.

Canadians are enthusiastic church members, and churches of all denominations are thriving social as well as religious centres. Perhaps it's fair to say that they are *more* social than religious. For in the suburbs the puritan heritage of the small town undergoes a curious mutation: the obsession with what is morally right becomes an obsession with what is hygienic. Gluttony, for instance, is obviously no longer one of the seven deadly sins; it is simply unhealthy. (Perhaps in revolt against the dismal science of dietetics, Canadian adolescents consume vast quantities of potato chips and tooth-rotting soft drinks.) It is the same with the other deadly sins. They are not so much problems for the minister as for the social worker.

The friendliness of Friendsville survives in the city. Even in surly Toronto, a man waiting in an icy wind for his bus is sometimes offered a lift.

IV

Canada is so intransigently regional that few generalizations about its national character are valid. All its citizens call themselves Canadian, yet the word means something different to each. 'Historically', Northrop Frye has said, 'a Canadian is an American who rejects the revolution.' This accounts for the descendants of the United Empire Loyalists, actual and spiritual, who fled the United States in order to continue living under the British Crown. It accounts too for those deeply religious French Canadians who reject the French Revolution. And it's true that both these groups have been influential in their own ways. An astute Canadian economist, Professor Harry Johnson of the University of Chicago, has written sarcastically of Canadian economic policy as having been 'historically dominated by the ambition to create a country rival in power to the United States, and so to prove that the Americans were wrong to revolt from colonial rule in 1776'. Yet many Canadians vigorously reject these negative traditions.

The truth is that the thought 'Canada' is impossible to think all at once. Love of country is difficult when, like Aristotle's 'creature of vast size – one, say, 1,000 miles long', its unity and wholeness are lost to imagination. And so the patriotism of Canadians tends to be – in a perfectly respectable and human sense – provincial, and even parochial.

The people of each region have their own character.

Maritimers are a seafaring race whose roots are deep in history. Canada is sometimes thought of (quite wrongly) as a 'new' country. The Maritime provinces belong essentially to the Old World. The things that surprise, enchant, and sometimes distress North American travellers in Europe are also to be found here: craftsmanship, tradition, cheerful poverty. A sense of history clings about the silvery weathered shingles of fishermen's huts; the vivid colours of boats and lobster floats – red, blue, ochre, green – and the black-and-white dazzle of painted wooden houses are affirmations of life and vigour against the hard grey weather and the dangerous ocean. Men have been here a long time; they have come to terms with the forests, the rocks, the tides. It was in 1605 that Samuel de Champlain planted Canada's first settlement at Port Royal – now Annapolis Royal, Nova Scotia. Not far away, at Pubnico, there are some eight hundred French-speaking Nova Scotians named D'Entremont. Most of them have the ascetic features of

V MILL ON THE RIDEAU RIVER, ONTARIO

the family face: they are all descended from the Sieur D'Entremont who landed here in 1650. St John's, Newfoundland, was first settled in 1613: its people retain the Jacobean turns of phrase, the ballads, the hearty manners of their ancestors.

Maritimers, many of them with the quick pride of Scots Highland descent, are touchy about the chronic depression of their region. Aware that their economy is to some extent subsidized from Central Canada, they resent 'Upper Canadians' and are fond of denouncing the frantic pace of life in Ontario compared with the pleasant, lethargic tempo of their own own existence.

French Canadians cherish their own mythology and defensive folklore. '*Je me souviens*', their motto, recalls the national trauma – the conquest of New France upon the Plains of Abraham before the walled city of Quebec. Since that fatal day, September 13, 1759, they have seen themselves as beleaguered champions of the Catholic faith and its guardian the French tongue in a continent predominantly American and Protestant. Henri Bourassa, most eloquent of Canadian orators, spoke for his nation when he cried out passionately at the Montreal Eucharistic Congress on September 6, 1910: 'Providence has willed that the principal group of this French and Catholic colonization should constitute in America a separate corner of the earth, where the social, religious, and political situation most closely approximates to that which the Church teaches us to be the ideal state of society. . . . But, it is said, you are only a handful; you are fatally destined to disappear; why persist in the struggle? We are only a handful, it is true; but in the school of Christ I did not learn to estimate right and moral forces by number and wealth. We are only a handful; but we count for what we are; and we have the right to live. . . .'

More than fifty years later the 'ideal state of society' of the devout *habitants* has disappeared and the French Canadians have become an urban proletariat. While the fragrant spirit of John XXIII has sweetened their faith, they have discovered their political strength and a new sense of purpose. By a paradox they have become most sharply aware of their distinctness at the very moment when they are becoming most 'American'.

The crooked streets of Quebec City cast their old spell, delightfully French-provincial in the shade of old trees in summer, antique as a Christmas-card under winter snow. In the citadel redcoats of the 22nd Foot wheel and stamp to orders shouted in the curiously nasal French of the province. *Monsieur le Président* (Mr Speaker) sits under the crucifix in the legislative assembly. A spectacled nun appears at the grille through which visitors are inter-viewed at the ancient Couvent des Ursulines; a moment later she returns to display with shy pride the skull of General Montcalm. But such impressions can be deceptive. The dark-haired girls, demure in their little black dresses, are North American women, capable, energetic, adventurous. And under the sober jacket of the young *séparatiste* hurrying to early Mass beats the heart of an automobile salesman.

All this is much more obvious in Montreal, the world's second biggest French-speaking city. This is the city which, above all others, has seized the affection of Canadians. Novel after novel has explored the intricate life of its streets and parks. Despite the bilingual signs and the brooding presence of huge, prison-like religious institutions, Montreal is plainly a New World city. Everyone here is cheerfully on the make. There is that sense (strong too in Toronto) that nothing is permanent. Buildings are constantly being torn down to be replaced by taller and richer ones, streets being ripped open for new sewers or subways, ambulances racing to the rescue of accident victims, sirens screaming, signs dazzling, merchandise being sacrificed to make way for the new line, the new model, the new chain-store – the whole exciting circus of planned obsolescence and competitive selling.

French Canadians are awaking to the knowledge that this is their world and their country. They have recognized their enemy in the 'Anglo-Saxon' *élite* who dominate Canada's economy. This *élite*, though stoutly entrenched in Montreal, whose commercial life it controls, has its spiritual home in Toronto.

One of the few shared sentiments of all regions of Canada is an unreasoning dislike of Toronto. Unreasoning, because the Toronto loathed throughout Canada has pretty well ceased to exist. The dour, philistine Orangemen who earned the city its unpleasant reputation have long been outnumbered by swarms of immigrants from Europe and from other parts of Canada. True, there's still a great parade down University Avenue on the glorious Twelfth of July, with drums and bands and orange sashes and even King Billy on his white charger. But the crowds who turn out to cheer are mostly Italians – everyone, after all, loves a band. For if Montreal is bicultural, Toronto is multicultural – an expanding, expansive metropolis which will soon have a population of two million. As Montreal is the centre of French-speaking Canadian life, Toronto is the hub of English Canada. Here are centred its publishing and communication industries, its commercial and financial empires, music, art, and theatre. Heavy industry is close by in Hamilton, and a third of Canada's population is concentrated in the rich farmlands and small cities of southern Ontario within a radius of three hundred miles.

Ontario people are sober, hard-working, orderly; as if to insist on their difference from the Americans they resemble so closely, they are strong for the Queen. The men tend to be serious about their work to the point of solemnity; at the same time they cherish the image of Huck Finn and are boyishly eager to head out for the bush. They are decent people, if – as they often complain themselves – a bit dull. And they are not nearly so hostile to French Canadians

VI FIELD OF RAPE, SOUTHERN SASKATCHEWAN

as the latter imagine: their reaction to Separatist agitation is to organize classes in French. Normally, of course, they do not think about Quebec; it simply doesn't impinge on their consciousness any more than Canada itself does on the mind of a New Yorker. For the only evidence of French Canada in Ontario (outside a few border communities) is the bilingual food-package: 'snap, crackle, pop' on one side of the cereal-carton becomes 'cric, crac, croc' on the other. It's hard to build understanding on evidence as flimsy as that.

The West begins at Winnipeg, a mystique of white Stetsons, 'man-size' beefsteaks, and back-slapping hospitality. There is a tendency, too, for the necktie to atrophy into a sort of halter of bootlaces. Ontario and Quebec and the Maritimes suddenly recede to a great distance not only in space but in time. Here they are 'the East'. The cities of Central Canada, which seem to the people who live in them so new and raw, from here take on the aspect of ancient centres of privilege and decorum, crusted with culture and learning. Wide, empty landscapes of bald prairie, oppressed by the enormous sky, wait at the limits of prairie cities. The company of fellow-men becomes vital. And in Alberta, as the flat prairie begins to undulate in ever shorter and steeper waves to the foothills of the Rockies, the company of God himself is sought by the people of the 'Bible belt'; not only in theocratic colonies of bearded, black-clad Hutterites, but in small, bleak churches and conventicles of innumerable fundamentalist sects.

British Columbia, cut off from the rest of Canada by range beyond range of enormous, uninhabitable mountains, lives its own life. British Columbians are the most American Canadians, farthest removed from bicultural compromises; they are also the most British. Life is pleasant in the mild green climate of the Coast. The mist comes down on the mountains and silent forests, the Pacific glimmers below – who needs Canada? 'As far as I'm concerned,' a British Columbian told me not long ago, 'the Atlantic Ocean might just as well be washing at the foot of the Rockies.' In the remote valleys of the Interior – as the hinterland of Vancouver is gallantly called – a few pilgrim souls, the last puritans, live by the light of conscience: Quakers, anarchists, pacifists, the unhappy Doukhobor Sons of Freedom. Cowboys ride the range on the high, semi-arid plateau of the Cariboo country. Loggers, miners, and fishermen earn the provincial income. But a good two-thirds of British Columbians are concentrated in the cities of Vancouver and Victoria where the living is easy, summer and winter.

People who do not know Canada sometimes think of it, as Voltaire did, as a few acres of snow.

It is, of course, a northern country. Over most of it the climate is one of violent extremes – swelteringly hot summers and Siberian winters. Arctic Canada – the true North – is almost uninhabited. There are only some eleven thousand Eskimoes. The other people of a few small, scattered communities like Churchill, Inuvik, and Aklavik live a frontier life with, at Inuvik, every modern convenience, including heated sewage. (Because of permafrost, drainpipes are above the surface, and have to be heated to avoid freezing.) Northerners regard the rest of Canada and indeed the rest of the world as 'Outside'.

There is still a powerful myth of the North. Against all evidence, Canadians sometimes like to think of themselves as a hardy, frugal race of *hommes du nord*. For the farther north one goes, the farther one is from the United States and from supermarkets, super-highways, and advertising-men in crew-cuts and two-button suits. One must suffer to be a Canadian (says the myth): here incomes are lower and prices higher than in the republic to the south: go north, young man. Canadians may not be particularly hardy, but they are hard-headed. They indulge this dream only at election-time and when they are on vacation.

V

Canada is a society rather than a nation. Its coherence depends on a communications system in which the radio and television networks of the Canadian Broadcasting Corporation play a supremely important part. There is no central and controlling myth to focus Canadian diversity and foster its distinctness. Canadians cannot agree on a national flag or a national anthem. The Crown, which in theory symbolizes the State, is an absentee landlord. Ottawa is a page in the geography book, a chapter of history.

But there is one definitive doctrine that runs through the whole of Canadian history and life and into the remotest parts of Canadian territory. The doctrine of the panacea of compromise has almost the force of a myth.

By compromise the fierce debates between English and French, between Catholic and Protestant, between Church and State, between public and private ownership, between Ottawa and the provinces have been mediated or side-tracked. In this way the peace has been kept between elements which are potentially hostile.

The great political parties, nominally Progressive Conservative and Liberal, are internally based on compromises so far-reaching that a Tory can easily be accommodated by the Liberals and a *laissez-faire* Liberal by the Conservatives. There is compromise everywhere. Should the railways be nationalized? Yes and no. Should there be commercial radio and television or a publicly owned system free of advertising? Yes and no. Is education the duty of the State or of the Church? It is the duty of both, of either and of neither. Should murderers be hanged? No – that is to say, yes, up to a point.

26

VII VICTORIA, BRITISH COLUMBIA

By compromise Canadians manage to have the best of all possible worlds, and the worst. Canadians manage to live together peaceably by minding their own business and staying in their own backyards. No attempt is made to indoctrinate immigrants or children with State myths. It is enough that they respect the State and keep the laws. And there is very little discrimination against anyone on the ground of colour, race, or creed.

But to mind one's own business may lead at last to lack of interest in other people. Canadians are little given to personal gossip. They get away from their fellows whenever possible to stare at lakes and trees and rocks. There are fewer good novels written in Canada (the novel being essentially concerned with Other People) and there is more good painting based on landscape than the country's state of civilization would lead one to expect. And the plight of some groups of Canadians – the Indians, for example, and the Negroes of Halifax County, whose condition is cruelly depressed – is a bitter demonstration that the habit of live-and-let-live may become a kind of indifference.

And yet it is a good country, a State which has come into existence peaceably and maintained its integrity with remarkably little shedding of blood. Rich and resourceful, it is an open society in which power is decentralized, a free country which has remained innocent of lawlessness and gang-rule. Hegelian ideas of the superiority of the State to the sum of its parts are so widely accepted that it may come as a surprise to find that here, where the State has become a sort of board of arbitrators, the human spirit flowers in quiet.

KILDARE DOBBS

VIII SKEENA RIVER TRIBUTARY, BRITISH COLUMBIA

NOTES ON THE PLATES

Notes on the plates by James W. Bacque

*Additional photographs for this book were supplied
by four Toronto photographers:
Ray Webber (Labrador), Horst Ehricht (Yukon)
Herbert Taylor (the High Arctic) and
George Hunter (Winnipeg)*

Colour Plates

I 'Rocky Mountain grass' is the name local people give to little trees such as these in the forests round PEYTO LAKE, ALBERTA (near the British Columbia border north of Banff). Species that reach above one hundred feet on the Coast are here, at the same age, stunted specimens sometimes not over twenty feet. From British Columbia's evergreen forests comes a huge annual harvest of timber and pulp worth, in 1962, $780 million – forty per cent of the province's gross product.

Much of the water along this flank of the Rockies is glacial, with the same clear green-blue colour as Peyto Lake. The Bow River pouring down from the mountains in spring shines a lovely clay-green, even in its shallow stretches.

On the left of this photograph is Mount Patterson, 10,490 feet. The time is five o'clock on a July morning; the direction: north-west.

II This piece of Atlantic shore, the point of Canada closest to Europe, is also the part first settled by Europeans (looking north-west from CAPE SPEAR toward St John's).

Bay Bulls, just south of here, dates from the days of the Welsh and Irish colonies in Newfoundland in the early seventeenth century. It was fought over furiously by English, French, and Dutch: at the parish church in the village are gateposts made from cannon left over from ancient wars. The last siege ended in 1796.

Sir George Calvert, the first Lord Baltimore, planted a colony on this peninsula in 1622. He named the land Avalon, which is now the name for the east peninsula of Newfoundland. Baltimore lived there with his family for several years, but the colony never prospered. After the final failure, he moved most of the people to Virginia, and the land was virtually empty for eight years, until taken over by the privateer Sir David Kirke. He lived there intermittently, supporting Charles I during the Cromwell régime, then returned and died there *c.* 1655. His tomb is said to be somewhere near Ferryland, at the south end of the Avalon Peninsula.

III After the woodland canoe, surely the most beautiful small boat in North America is the graceful dory of Nova Scotia. These sixteen-footers, at rest in late afternoon in MAHONE BAY, NEAR BLUE ROCKS, NOVA SCOTIA, come from generations of experience with the sea, all the curves so beautifully adapted to wind and wave that men have ridden out full gales embraced by them. The boats are all hand-built, lap-streak, and with flat bottoms, which makes them easy to row – and stack. Children learn the ways of boats and the sea rowing around little fishing coves such as this one: their fathers take the dories to sea nested four to six deep on the decks of fishing schooners. On the Banks, they row out, two to a boat, to hand-line for cod. If they are separated from the mother-ship by a gale, they throw out a sea-anchor, lash a pole from the high-flaring bow to the high-flaring stern, fasten a tarpaulin down like a tent over their heads to cover the boat completely, and ride it out.

The fish-houses, built either on rock-filled cribs or on mortared stone foundations, are sited at the edge of the low-tide mark, and built to stand above high tide, so the boats can be launched or docked at any tide. In these buildings the fishermen land their catch, and here they clean, salt, dry, and flake them. Often the houses are used to store the fish as well.

IV The car-exhausts plume out like squirrel-tails, the brake-lights glitter, galoshes squeak on slivers of snow, and MONTREAL heads into another winter evening of twenty or thirty below. Along these short side-streets – Stanley, Metcalfe, and Peel, looking south-west from Sherbrooke Street to Dorchester – the traffic freezes solid on a winter evening, and the air flowing down from the side of the mountain is so pure and cold that it seems to have come unchanged from the high Arctic. There is a special excitement about this kind of dark cold. In the words of Montrealer Hugh MacLennan: 'It was exciting on the campus with the sound of creaking feet as the students hurried past clamping their ears; there was the recurrent excitement an extremely cold night gives in Canada.

33

The evening star was yellow in a tiny green corona caught in a net of bare branches . . .' (from *The Watch That Ends the Night*). The campus is McGill, just north of these side-streets. In the distance, the tall shaft of the Canadian Imperial Bank of Commerce Building, bright with the last blaze of the sun, will shine on for half an hour or more after the dropping sun has left the streets below to night.

V One of the first luxuries of life to arrive in pioneer Upper Canada was a mill such as this one on the RIDEAU RIVER system. The first mills seemed luxuries, because in the early nineteenth century grinding your own grain day by day in a coffee mill, or similar primitive machine, was tedious and inefficient. Water-powered mills were built within a few years after the founding of a settlement, often with Government help. At first the small, primitive mills were hardly profitable, especially competing against flour imported under low tolls. Later in the century, when there was a domestic surplus of wheat, many of the old grist mills were converted into 'merchant flour mills' grinding flour for export. A moderate-sized mill with several 'run of stones' (grindstones) could produce more than one hundred barrels a day. Steam, and later Diesel, power replaced the water-powered mills. A few still operate in Ontario, notably at Canton, near Port Hope.

Some mills, including this one, have been converted to residences. The seclusion, the sound of running water near by, and a view over a large pond which has had time to grow into the landscape attract painters, sculptors, cottagers, fishermen.

VI A mile off the Trans-Canada Highway in southern SASKATCHEWAN, on a calm morning in June, this field of rape lies simmering in the hot, bright sun. This is the best part of the year on the prairies. The rivers are full, the birds sing over the unfenced fields, the white-grey country roads unwind ahead, smooth and dustless. At the end of a day like this one, in the beautiful description by W. O. Mitchell, '. . . shadows lengthen; the sunlight fades from cloud to cloud, kindling their torn edges as it dies from softness to

softness down the prairie sky. A lone farmhouse window briefly blazes; the prairie bathes in mellower, yellower light, and the sinking sun becomes a low and golden glowing, splendid on the prairie's edge.' (From *Who Has Seen the Wind*.)

VII VICTORIA, BRITISH COLUMBIA, is like Mr Kildare Dobbs's Friendsville (see page 13) – a tidy town with gentle people. Everything is easygoing here. Under its seasonal haze the town drifts through a long, mild summer (the yellow haze lying under the clouds is late summer forest-fire smoke). The seasons transfer gently, not in days or weeks, but through months. The climate is invariably mild: there have been winters without a single frost and all kinds of bizarre southern trees are indigenous – the smooth-shanked arbutus, Garry oak, cascara, western yew, and others not found elsewhere in Canada.

This view, on an August evening from Summit Lookout in Mount Tolmie Park, faces west over the northern part of the city.

VIII Flooding in spring, this creek in northern BRITISH COLUMBIA breaks its snowy banks on its way to the master stream, the Skeena River, which flows to the Pacific Ocean just south of Prince Rupert. The Skeena and its tributaries support huge runs of salmon and trout: in the ponds of such tributaries as this, the water itself seems to turn pink at spawning time when the fish crowd over the gravel. The eulachon, or candlefish, also spawns in this area. It is so oily that the Tsimshian Indians used to dry the little fish, thread a wick through it, and light it as a candle.

This stream is on the dividing-line between British Columbia's two major forest zones: the coastal to the west, where the trees grow huge and stand densely packed, and the interior zone to the east, where the trees are small and more scattered. The coast, with its warm, wet climate, supports variety as well as magnificence and abundance. Inland, where the winters are arctically cold and rainfall is light, the forests include only the standard Canadian northern trees – tamarack, spruce, fir, birch, poplar.

1–5 The south shore and the Gaspé region, forming the long lower lip of the ST LAWRENCE RIVER, edge the river and the gulf in a smooth curve ending in the Baie des Chaleurs. It is all a rural, peaceful country, largely French-speaking, and poor through the Gaspé.

The little towns (such as Les Méchins, plate 1) straddle the road that runs for hundreds of miles within sight and scent of the St Lawrence. About 400,000 people live here in the settled strip, which is about 330 miles long and thirty to eighty miles wide. Inland are the hills, scarcely inhabited, rising to their peak at Mont Jacques Cartier, 4,160 feet. The names of the south shore and Gaspé are memorable: St Jean Port Joli, Val Brillant, Shickshock Mountains.

The centre of village life has for centuries been the church – in fact, the people think not so much of villages or areas as of parishes. The steeples sheathed in tin or, lately, aluminium, shine over dozens of valley and seaside villages through the area.

Summer is Gaspé's great season: the painters, anglers, travellers, and politicians are back, talking and spending. The valleys shine, the weather is good, the roads passable. Winter is a yearly disaster. The storms close off the roads, and the men work for a pittance in the woods (sometimes not even earning enough to pay for the chain-saws they must buy), or else they go on relief. For weeks some of the back-roads are plugged with drifts higher than the phone poles, and the temperature itself seems frozen at twenty or thirty below zero F. Spring is as sudden as the stoop of a hawk, and violent: foundations and roads heave and buckle as four or five feet of frost come out; conflicting gales twist the pines; the hillsides shed tons of meltwater and rain into creeks throttled with ice; bridges collapse. But the people sigh with relief, make their maple syrup, and go fishing for the Gaspé salmon.

The photographs, taken in November, catch the country in a cool mood, the fields shaven, the roads not yet walled with their customary winter drifts, the creeks open. The villages, Les Méchins (plate 1), St Yvon (plates 2 and 4), Grande Vallée (plate 3), and Mont Louis (plate 5), lie around the north-east end of the Gaspé lip.

6–8 The farming country inland from the Bay of Fundy, behind the hills of SUSSEX in New Brunswick, settles in November to a quiet season, the big barns rustling with the dairy cattle. The poet Charles Bruce found the atmosphere of this scene:

> This is the season when the darkest grass
> Flows in its deepest waves, on fading stubble;
> The time of cloud; and cattle brought to stable
> At dusk; and moonlit water still as glass . . .
> (From 'Fall Grass' in *The Mulgrave Road*.)

In November, this country is on the edge of a cyclonic winter. Lying on the east rim of the vast continent, it suffers the inflow of cold polar air masses from the north-west. It is also near the Bay of Fundy, whose warming influence keeps the January mean at a tolerable twenty degrees F. But it is this juxtaposition that keeps the weather cyclonic, for along the edge of the continent run terrible storms during winter, as the masses of Arctic air beat at the warm air of the sea.

9–19 Nova Scotia, which has been characterized as an island joined to Canada by a narrow peninsula of resentment, has in fact given the nation three Prime Ministers, many of the country's finest authors, and countless academics and businessmen. The province, like Britain and New England, the ancient lands of its people, is dented and cut by the sea: no part of it is more than forty-five miles from high tide. LUNENBURG (plates 9–19), along with dozens of other ports, coves, bays, and harbours round the coast, still sends its men to sea in ships. Nearly 8,000 men of this coast take their living from the sea.

The dragger (plate 13) literally drags a tremendous iron-mouthed net along the bottom of the sea, catching whatever is there. The winch lifts the net (plate 10) aboard, and the fishermen take what they want – cod flounder, plaice, redfish – and topple the rest back. Often other species are ground into fish-meal. What they catch is worth $20 million on the average each year, eighty per cent of Nova Scotia's total. Their boats – draggers, trawlers, long-liners – number over 5,000, and their skills and songs are now part of a way of life that changes very slowly. Lunenburg, home of the original fast fishing schooner *Bluenose*, has still so many men skilled at wooden-ship building that she lately launched an exact replica of the *Bluenose*. When the producers of the film *Mutiny on the Bounty* needed a replica of the eighteenth-century Royal Navy vessel, they went not to England but to Smith and Rhuland at Lunenburg (plate 14 left). Lunenburgers also build swordfishermen (plate 14 right) and, of course, dories (plate 12). Although some of the fishing boats are made with hand-adzed wood frames (plate 11), as they have been since before the American Revolution, the larger ones today are usually made of steel. The common food, and export, salt cod, is unloaded from a Newfoundland fishing schooner (plate 9) at a Lunenburg dock.

The sea that shapes the lives in the ports tempers the climate all over the province. After the Pacific Coast and southern Ontario, Nova Scotia is the warmest part of Canada. Halifax is, next to Vancouver, the wettest big city in Canada, with fifty-four inches of precipitation yearly, never less than three and a half inches in a month.

The narrow, hilly streets of Lunenburg are lined with houses like these (plates 15–17): chimneys up the middle, clapboard siding, painted white and trimmed with black, and tall windows lighting high rooms.

St John's Anglican Church (plate 18), founded in 1753, is entirely wooden. Wood has dominated Nova Scotia – in the houses, the ships, even the graveyards (plate 19), where some of the 'headstones' are in fact 'headboards'.

20–22   Listen – the ceaseless cadence, deep and slow.
Tomorrow. Now. And years and years ago.
The last lines of Charles Bruce's poem 'Eastern Shore' summarize the round of time and weather in MAHONE BAY (plate 20). The town of Mahone Bay (plate 21), tranquil and slow, seems to fit the lines as well. Shipbuilders trained here in the old Nova Scotia traditions export small plywood or plank outboard hulls all over North America.

The centre of industry and transportation in Nova Scotia is its capital HALIFAX, and Bedford Basin (plate 22) with its tankers and warships is one of the busiest shipping areas in Canada (sixth in total tonnage in 1960). The city itself, foggy, old, and quiet, has lately been changing. A new automobile factory has been set up across the harbour at near-by Dartmouth; industry has expanded and found new markets; drama has had a revival under Canadian directors and playwrights. The old hopes of Nova Scotia are beginning to materialize in action.

23–29   Fishermen's boxy wood houses stagger down the east edge of Canada (plate 23) overlooking the harbour entrance of ST JOHN'S, Newfoundland. The outlook here is quiet and hopeful. The people are not rich, but few of them are poor in the sense of lacking essentials of any kind. The air is clean, the views are magnificent, and a man with a boat is a man with good health and an escape from his depressions. It is completely appropriate that the tune of a favourite old Newfoundland reel is lively and happy. The words are:

> I'se the bye that builds the boat
> And I'se the bye that sails her
> And I'se the bye that catches the fish
> And brings them home to Li-zer.

The attitude is independent, and the tune is sassy. Most of the men who live in this section of St John's, the Upper Battery, are fishermen, and 'Li-zer' is not only used to seeing her husband's long-liner go out after cod from the harbour entrance (plate 29 top) but is ready to help clean, cook, or sell the catch (plates 24, 25).

St John's is one of the oldest cities in North America, first settled by Devonshire fishermen early in the sixteenth century, about one hundred years before the Quebec and Virginia settlements. French, English, Basque, and Portuguese used to fish the Grand Banks, and shelter here. It was of this bay behind its famous headlands that the Sieur de Roberval wrote, in the *Voyages, Navigations, Traffiques and Discoveries of the English Nation*: '. . . wee could not reach Newfound lande, untill the seventhe of June [1542]. The eight of the month, wee entred into the Rode of Saint John, where wee founde seventeene Shippes of fishers. While wee made somewhat long abode here, Jacques Cartier and his company returning from Canada, whither he was sent with five sayles the yeere before, arrived in the very same harbour. . . .'

The fishermen of today's St John's live in the Batteries – Upper (plate 23), Lower, and Outer – so named because guns used to be mounted here to defend St John's and the harbour (plates 28, 29) against, at different times, Englishmen, Frenchmen, Spaniards, and pirates.

Signal Hill (plate 27), where this stone ruin stands, overlooks St John's Harbour, and is included in Signal Hill National Park. Here, in 1901, Marconi received the first transatlantic radio message, and here, during centuries before, Newfoundlanders watching for enemies approaching the harbour prepared to shell them from stone forts.

Near Sugar Loaf Head (plate 26), or the Sugar-loaf, just north of St John's, is a prime fishing ground for long-liners from St John's.

For all its apparent devotion to tradition, New-foundland has changed profoundly since confederation with Canada in 1949. Fishing has shrunk in import-ance until it now accounts for only ten per cent of the island's income: 500 new schools have been built since 1949 and 945 rebuilt; 1,600 miles of new road have been constructed, and 1,500 rebuilt; the infant and maternal mortality rates have both dropped signi-ficantly.

Life has been imitating the artist in Newfoundland in at least one instance: forty years later, the province followed its great poet, E. J. Pratt, into Canada. Pratt, who graduated from Victoria College in Toronto in 1911, lived there the rest of his life, but his lyric poems are chiefly of Newfoundland – 'The Toll of the Bells' illustrates the sadness of the sailors' death:

We gave them at the harbour every token –
The ritual of the guns, and at the mast
The flag half-high, and as the cortege passed
All that remained by our dumb hearts unspoken.

(From *Collected Poems* by E. J. Pratt.)

30-32 LABRADOR, to most Canadians, is a word like heaven, with definite meaning, and no particular geography. They would rather like to see it, but the

chances seem remote. They are vaguely aware of a long strip of land up the east end of the country, and some inlets. That is about all. From the point of view of Penthouse Man, there is nothing more. He is happy to read about it incidentally in E. J. Pratt's lines in *The Titanic*, describing the birth and drift of an iceberg:

Calved from a glacier near Godhaven coast,
It left the fjord for the sea – a host
Of white flotillas gathering in its wake . . .
. . . No smoke
Of steamships nor the hoist of mainsails broke
The polar wastes – no sounds except the grind
Of ice, the cry of curlews and the lore
Of winds from mesas of eternal snow:
Until caught by the western undertow
It struck the current of the Labrador . . .

This current, sweeping down from the Arctic Ocean, keeps coastal Labrador fog-bound or frozen during most of the year. The settlements have a mix-ture of people: English-Scots immigrants whose ancestors arrived in the nineteenth century, Eskimoes, and Naskapi Indians (plate 30, paddling out the North West River at Lake Melville near the settle-ment of North West River).

Part of the Algonkian group, the Naskapi range over all of the Labrador peninsula, from the St Lawrence to Ungava, from Hudson Bay to the Atlantic. In the southern part, round settlements such as North West River, the caribou are nearly gone, and the Indians have little to live on. They hunt in winter and fish in summer, but the results are so poor that much of their food, clothing, and shelter is charity, given by the government of Newfoundland, or such missions as the Oblate Fathers.

Where they are close to white men's influence, the Indians are slowly losing their traditions and hunting-songs. Many of the traditional crafts and songs are spurned by young Indians trying to learn the white man's ways. Their numbers are increasing, in common with all Canadian Indians today. This is due partly to food, which, if debilitating, is at least regular, and to early treatment for tuberculosis. Their canoes (plate 30) are canvas on wood now: the canvas is imported and the wood frames they make themselves. The paddles are spruce, home-made.

At Davis Inlet (plate 31) farther up the coast, the Naskapi come to buy food and clothing. They use wooden one-cylinder putt-putts largely made in Toronto or Montreal. From these boats, they are learning to fish for cod, sea-trout, and salmon.

Joe Rich, of the Davis Inlet band, tells a story to family and friends in his hunting tent (plate 32) set up specially for the photographer. Hunting tents are usually of caribou skin stretched on spruce poles, but this one was made of old blankets and parachute silk. Spruce branches hold down the floppy material, tied together with strings made out of roots.

Used to walking long distances over their rocky and hilly country in search of game, these Indians, like their inland relatives generations ago, have an amazingly accurate sense of place. Any hunter can quickly draw a precise map of hundreds of square miles of his territory. Their powers of endurance are remarkable: they commonly cover forty miles in a day on foot, and one woman recently walked eighteen miles to have her baby baptized. It was three days old when she set out.

Inland from these people, Labrador is alive with the sound of helicopters and iron-ore trains in the mountains and river valleys. Engineers are chopping sight-lines down the steep banks of the Hamilton River, and at night in their tents behind the mosquito-netting they work out the power available from the generating plants they will build on the river's magnificent falls (360,000 horsepower at Hamilton Falls alone). Already, the Quebec, Newfoundland, and Federal governments are embroiled in disputes about sovereignty over the Indians and Eskimoes, about off-shore islands, and about the border between the provinces; already the town of Sept Iles, which did not exist a few years ago, is the third largest port in Canada in terms of tonnage handled. All its business is to or from the iron-mines at Knob Lake on the Labrador-Quebec border.

33-40 This part of the St Lawrence, backed by long hills (plate 33), is perhaps the best-known stretch of river in Canada: it has certainly stirred the emotions of millions of immigrants, travellers, and returning Canadian soldiers, in sailing ships and liners, arriving to anchor here or passing up-river almost with the feeling of obeisance. The east windows of the turreted Château Frontenac Hotel look out over the Lower Town and harbour, over the Beauport shore (right) and Ile d'Orléans, the classic view from ancient QUEBEC. The hills to the north-east (background) are the beginning of a tremendous hinterland that stretches, lightly inhabited, to the Lake St John country, and from there on, virtually deserted, to the shores of the Arctic Ocean at Davis Strait. If Quebec is the first sight of metropolitan Canada for the returning traveller on board ship, it is the last for the prospector, lumberman, or geophysicist heading into the bush and muskeg of northern Quebec.

Quebec City's pre-eminence in Canadian life is a matter of prestige, antiquity, and sentiment: she has not much large industry except her governments – provincial and ecclesiastic. (Gross annual production in the city averages $300 million.) Quebec is by Canadian standards a middling city (the metropolitan area included 357,000 people in 1961, sixth in Canada; the city proper had 171,000, ninth in Canada), but it is focus and symbol for French North Americans from Louisiana to Ungava, and to many of the five and a half million French Canadians it is more personal and more important than Ottawa. This St Lawrence aspect of the French citadel (plate 33) has inspired artists, including J. W. Morrice, who painted views of the Lévis ferry about 1905. The streets – Champlain (plate 35), St Louis (plate 36), and St Flavien (plate 39) – and the boardwalk on the Dufferin Terrace (plate 40) have inspired novelists, notably Roger Lemelin, whose good-natured Lower Town characters have assumed a place in French-Canadian literature and folk-lore. Notre-Dame-de-Québec (plate 37) and the Château Frontenac (plate 34) are pre-eminent in the city, which, considering its early founding, has surprisingly few ancient buildings surviving whole. Most of the old buildings were destroyed or heavily damaged by fire or by artillery.

Notre-Dame-de-Québec is a basilica, dating from the middle of the eighteenth century. The interior, theatrical in its grandeur, was executed between 1780 and 1800 by the Baillargés, a family of architects, sculptors, and wood-carvers.

Quebec stands clearly superior in its own mind to compromising, erratic, effervescent Montreal, and the proof is partly in the purity and ancient form of its French. 'Tabagie' on the sign over a tobacconist's (plate 38) is a word unused in Montreal, where they say 'Tabac'. Such modernisms are frowned on by the purists of Quebec, who contend, with support from educated Parisians, that the French language at the city's Laval University is in a better state than French anywhere else in the world.

41-46 SOUTH AND WEST OF QUEBEC CITY, stretching up the St Lawrence, is a pocket of fertile land bordered by the foothills of the Appalachian Mountains. Chiefly rural, with an increasing number of secondary industries, the country, especially in the Eastern Townships nearer Montreal, has been taken up only recently by French settlers. They moved out from the St Lawrence shore during the mid nineteenth century in a colonization drive that was partly competition with the English Canadians. Thus the names all through here, though predominantly French, are mixed: St Hyacinthe, Cowansville, Disraeli, Iberville – with aboriginal compromises such as Mégantic, Memphramagog. But names prove little except a mixed history – a town with an English name may be predominantly French, and vice versa.

The settlers took with them their seigneurial attitudes to land, and divided the country into strips marked by snake fences made of the felled timbers. Behind these ancient wooden fences (plate 41) there may stand a micro-wave relay tower.

Autumn comes early to the uplands near Quebec City, with overnight snows that melt at morning (plates 42, 43), but farther south, near the lakes and lower, the hardwood bush (plate 44) shines red, gold, and brown, for over a month. Among them, like the blackness of a photograph slowly appearing in the acid, come forward the green-black pines, spruces, and cedars.

'A hardwood copse in the Eastern Townships of Quebec in Indian summer can be compared to nothing else on earth, being itself an absolute. . . . After the first frost has turned ferns to brown dust and the birds have flocked south, the woods around my house in the country are filled with the living presence of silence.' (From *Scotchman's Return and Other Essays* by Hugh MacLennan.)

There is a moment in early spring that is exactly like this moment in fall: the air is still, the crows are squawking, the tree-shadows lie pale over a light ground. It was this moment in a copse such as this (plate 45) in the Eastern Townships that A. Y. Jackson painted in his *The Edge of the Maple Wood* (National Gallery of Canada), one of the most beautiful of all Canadian landscapes.

Cut-stone churches with tin roofs (plate 46) stand in scores of villages throughout this countryside. The wooden side-door is used on the coldest days in winter, when the front doors would be too draughty. These churches are closely related in style to the earlier buildings on the Ile d'Orléans near Quebec City: the church at Ste Famille there, for instance, with its corner belfries, is an obvious precursor in style of this Eastern Townships specimen.

47-58 The words of the fine French-Canadian poet Saint-Denys Garneau frame one view of MONTREAL:

> I walk beside a joy,
> A joy which is not for me.

Different, but close, like the statue of Charity (plate 47) beside the citadel of commerce (Canadian Imperial Bank of Commerce Building), the elements of Montreal stream along side by side, seldom mixing. Catholic, Protestant, Jew; French Canadian, English Canadian, New Canadian; Separatist, Federalist – the tinctures of difference are unending. The area round Place Ville Marie is almost the only common ground – apart from the Forum, the Art Gallery, and the Symphony – where something does not divide one citizen from another. The newsboys and most of the salespeople here – on Dorchester (plate 51), St Catherine (at Peel, plate 52), and Beaver Hall Hill (plate 53) – have an uncanny knack for telling a customer's language before he speaks, judging from a coat, a look, a haircut, perhaps even a man's gait.

Where the two cultures do touch intimately, however, there is likely to be the light and force of fusion. In certain regiments, including the Fusiliers Mont Royal, at both the great universities, Montréal and McGill, in the C.B.C. and the National Film Board, in the *boîtes*, and especially among painters and writers, there have been brilliant signs of the advantages of cultural disunity. The women of Montreal, benefiting from both cultures through marriage, ancestry, or friendship, are the most attractive and charming in the country.

Place Ville Marie, by far the most spectacular downtown development in Canada since the boom of the twenties, stands cold, tall, and regular in the middle of the most valuable real estate in the city. The development covers seven acres of land, houses the head offices of several big Canadian enterprises, and has spurred development of other blocks down town. Its inhuman regularity and size stand almost as if accused by the row of stone apostles on top of the Cathedral of Mary Queen of the World (plates 48 and 55), seat of the Catholic Archbishop of Montreal, Cardinal Léger.

Threatened by the enormous development all around are the small buildings, formerly houses, along such streets as Metcalfe (plates 49, 51), Stanley, and McTavish. These small cross-streets house restaurants, little art galleries, book stores (some bilingual), and boutiques, as well as some doubtful night clubs and antique stores.

Parc Lafontaine (plate 54), in the middle of the French and bourgeois east end of Montreal, is usually littered with students from the school that stands at the south end of the grounds. The park, divided by the Avenue Calixa Lavallée, contains a big track-and-field ground in the east half, and a lagoon in the west, complete with swans, bridge, and bun-eating ducks.

Beaver Hall Hill (plate 53), now a gutter of traffic between immense curbs of stone and glass, would astonish the fur-hatted, fur-trading men who gave the street its name. One of them, Joseph Frobisher, built here about the last decade of the eighteenth century a log house eighty feet long by thirty-six wide. Here came his Canadian partners and friends, talking of the vast enterprise that soon traded or explored as far away as the Arctic and Pacific shores of Canada.

The country that these men opened and exploited is nearly all deserted now: modern Canada, following the east–west routes they pioneered from Montreal, has turned south from them to build her cities and farms. The original canoe routes west from Montreal followed the southern boundary of the Canadian Shield all the way to the Athabaska territory, crossing the Shield at Lake Nipissing and at the Superior–Red River route. So important has this route been in history that most Canadians today still imagine that they are a Shield people, when in fact not a single one of the fourteen biggest cities stands on Shield rock. Most of those cities, such as Toronto and Vancouver, are far distant from the Shield; only two (Quebec and Ottawa) stand even within sight of the Canadian Shield hills. But large parts of the old trade routes are still in use: down the Great Lakes to Montreal, and thence across all the oceans. Much of the trans-shipping is at Montreal docks (loading grain brought east by rail, plate 57), but there is a large direct-freight traffic via the St Lawrence Seaway (St Lambert Lock, plate 56).

From St Helen's Island, just south of Montreal Island proper, the changing skyline of Montreal (plate 58) stands as it was in 1963, when the World's Fair planning was at its height and St Helen's Island was being ringed with ice-breaking dikes and artificial extensions. The southern leg of the new subway was projected to come almost directly towards the camera from the central massif of down town. Apart from the usual objectors to any grand scheme, there was one unlikely source of opposition to St Helen's as the World's Fair site – bird-watchers. The shore and water birds that enlivened the Montreal waterfront were all threatened, and many were left homeless by the bulldozers.

59–63 Standing waves of white water face up-stream in the Lachine rapids (plate 61), along the Montreal riverfront. They were first by-passed in 1825 by a canal with seven locks and a depth of five feet. Today, the SEAWAY CANAL along the south shore from Montreal to Caughnawaga is twenty miles long with two locks whose minimum dimensions are 766 feet (length) by 80 feet (breadth) by 30 feet (depth). The construction of the Seaway and the accompanying hydro-power developments meant the flooding of large areas (plate 59) between Lake Ontario and Montreal. From the air can still be seen the outline of old highways and canals under the water. This destruction of settled lands in eastern Ontario prompted the Ontario government to move or reconstruct and restore historic old houses in its Upper Canada Village near Morrisburg (plates 64–66).

An earlier wave of canal-building, prompted not by commercial necessity but by military needs, resulted in the joining of the Ottawa River with Lake Ontario via the Rideau and Cataraqui rivers in 1832. Together with locks on the Ottawa, the Rideau Canal (plate 60) provided between Montreal and the Great Lakes a water route safer from American attack than the direct St Lawrence passage. Soon after 1832, however, the British-American rivalry in North America had passed out of the military stage, and the Rideau has since become an attraction for tourists in cabin cruisers, many of them Americans.

The river that made Montreal, and helped to make Ottawa and much of Quebec province, flows out of Lake Ontario and past Cornwall (plates 62, 63), sadly polluted in its passage down by the riverside towns. Past the paper mills at Cornwall (seen in reflection, plate 63) and under the International Bridge there (plate 62) it slides, stained round the banks with algae and drifting garbage. The Ontario government, concerned about the loss of water resources through pollution, has set up the Ontario Water Resources Commission to help all municipalities clean up this kind of mess, and improvements are beginning to show in communities all along the Great Lakes system.

64–66 All men love the old house, roofed with brown,
    Rising grayly from its woodland ring,
  Over all the valley, ford and town,
    Facing westward like an agèd king . . .

  Into silent glades and leafy places
    Footsteps follow where the quiet flies –
  Sunlight scattered upon restful faces
    Shadows fallen upon pensive eyes. . . .
    Voices sweet
      Ebb and flow:
    Quiet feet
      Come and go
And among the faded stalks and ruined roses
The easy master of the house reposes.

      (From *The Poems of Archibald Lampman*.)

Lampman has expressed part of the reason why the Ontario government was concerned about the destruction of ancient homesteads, churches, and houses during construction of the St Lawrence Seaway. Buildings from the areas to be flooded were brought with a variety of others to make a village near Morrisburg with streets, mill, river – an atmosphere of its own – in the style of 1867. The houses are in clapboard (the French/Robertson house, plate 64), vertical siding, dressed stone (the Loucks house, plate 65), locally made brick, and squared logs (the hired man's house, plate 66). The buildings date from 1784 through the nineteenth century, but most have been restored to 1867 or a little before.

The French/Robertson house (plate 64) was built by Jeremiah French, who left Vermont about 1786 and built his first house here of frame. Later it was extended, and covered in clapboard. In front is an early door-yard garden. In the words of an early Scots gardener in Ontario: 'My flowers are very fine hollyhocks grown from seed I brought with me. Mignonette fills the air with sweetness, a grove of fine sunflowers and scarlet runners is in front of the house. I assure you it looks quite gay. . . .'

The garden of the hired man's house (plate 66) is extensive. Behind the three-rail, double-post-and-yoke fence are lilac, yellow burnet, rose, and pelargonium, among many other flowers. Behind the house is a large vegetable bed. The tree at right, an apple, is just finishing bearing, and the young whip before the left-hand window has recently been transplanted. A sheaf of drying corn frames the photograph on the left.

The eavestroughs of the house are made of wood, and the chimney and fireplace are of stone. Typically, these houses had a kitchen, a living-room, and two bedrooms downstairs, with a sleeping-loft above. Inside, this house is plastered and papered.

The Loucks house (plate 65) did not have fireplaces (note chimneys) but was heated by stoves, with a complete system of immense heat holes in the inside walls to circulate the warm air. There is a storage basement under the house, from which a dumb-waiter ascends to transport the cooled foods upstairs.

67–70 To these old buildings, men in beaver hats come to legislate. Their breath smoking as they cross from the

Château Laurier Hotel (next to the East Block of Parliament, from which plate 67 was photographed) after dinner for the evening debate, they have a moment's dark resemblance to their ancestors and predecessors, who paddled the Ottawa River (in the background) to buy beaver for fur caps. The shapes around them, the stone walls that echo their feet stamping off the snow, are older than the nation they govern.

The cornerstone of the first PARLIAMENT BUILDING was laid in 1860 by Edward, Prince of Wales. It was in a style similar to the romantic style of the West Block (plates 67, left, and 68), and there were drinking- and smoking-rooms for the M.P.s. Then the fire of 1916 destroyed the roof, floors, and parts of the walls of the original Centre Block. It was rebuilt, but in a simpler and more august style. The smoking-rooms, the drinking-rooms, and the fancy vanished together. Government buildings today, like government itself, are bigger, cleaner, and less imaginative than under Victoria. Hardly an architect in the world today, especially in Canada, would dare design something as frilly as the finial (plate 68) shaped in wrought iron like a fleur-de-lis, or the fussy, typically mid-Victorian iron cresting atop the West Block (plate 70).

The Centre Block itself is a sizeable but not over-powering building. The proportions of the original tower were improved in the reconstruction (designed by John Pearson), and a storey was added. There are now 490 rooms in the building, which measures 470 by 235 feet. The tower, 291 feet high, carries a fifty-three-bell carillon.

The Library of Parliament (behind the Centre Block), which was saved from the 1916 fire by an iron door in the corridor, was itself damaged by fire in 1952, and then restored. It was inspired by the Gothic chapter-house – the style is an over-elaborated example of Middle Gothic, especially on the exterior. Normally, the circular shape is not successful for a library, although two famous circular libraries – the British Museum Reading Room and the Radcliffe Camera at Oxford – continue despite the inherent difficulties of noise and cramped stack space.

71-75 The countryside south of Ottawa (plates 71-5), grown dry and slow with late summer, is too hot for field-work in the early afternoon, and all the farmers take an hour's siesta in the hammock on the lawn after lunch.

> Beyond them are great elms and poplar trees
> That guard the noon-stilled farm-yards, groves
> of pine,
> And long dark fences muffled thick with vine . . .

That was Lampman's description of a countryside like this in the 1890s. The roads are wider now, but the elms still stand over them.

Although it is still only August, some of the sumacs (plate 74) are beginning to turn red. The great maples (plate 73) can remain green and full-leafed right into October. The barns (plate 75) are typically hip-roofed and, by this season, loaded with carefully mowed hay, usually timothy. This crop is followed often by a second crop, of alfalfa, which grows below the hay in the same field and is harvested later. This year's thrashing is over and the baled straw is stacked outdoors in the barnyard to the left. The hardwoods here (plate 71), photographed in September, are beginning to show the contrasts of autumn; the milk-weed pods (at fence) are loaded with seedy, soft down.

Old habits linger among the farmers. Many of them keep unneeded horses in the barn although they have tractors and cars in the drive-sheds, and you will hear them refer to the 'hind' wheels of their cars.

76-78 Three buildings from the BROCKVILLE of the late nineteenth century show the taste of the Canadian Loyalist and Scots builders for medieval fantasy (note the spires of the church, plate 78; tower of the house, plate 76) and for the English Baroque. The church is a fairly characteristic example of Late Victorian Gothic. The limestone walls are rockface (that is, finished roughly, with an artificial bulge to simulate natural rock, in the manner of the Greek rustication). The City Hall, built in the fifties, is relatively smoothly dressed and shares with many Ontario public buildings of the time the influence of the English Baroque. The upper walls are hammer-dressed, and the basement and portals are rockface. The outline of the cupola is slightly Baroque, and a purist would probably insist that the clock-faced dormers are too large for the building.

The house (plate 76) was probably built about 1870–80 and is eclectic medieval in style. This style was extensively used, in wood, for summer cottages in the Thousand Islands area of the Upper St Lawrence River, near by.

79 KINGSTON, on the site of the ancient Fort Frontenac, outpost of the early French régime in Canada, has been fort, fur-trading-post, naval base, legislative seat, and university town. Here, built on Point Frederick on the east edge of the city, and viewed over the martello tower of the old Fort Henry (plate 79, right) is the Royal Military College. Founded in 1875, the College now trains officers for all three services. It is built mainly of Kingston limestone. The towered stone building at right is the headquarters of the College; at the left, the building with the porch near the water (Deadman's Bay) is the old 'stone frigate', built long before the College for naval stores. Just projecting above the building next left is the top of a stone martello tower at Fort Frederick, similar to the one at Fort Henry. The nearer tower is thicker on the seaward side than on the landward, so that, if threatened with capture, the defenders could turn their cannon and blow out the landward wall, making the tower useless.

80–85 From a Tory, Orange, loyal, shirt-sleeved sort of a burg, as it was in the thirties, TORONTO has changed into a North American metropolis that is on the verge of becoming an international city. In certain fields – music, commerce – the city has already broken clear of the old provincialism of which visitors have always accused it. Toronto is an excellent jazz city: it has more musicians, night clubs, good audiences, and experimental experts (the Advanced School of Contemporary Music is located there) than any city except New York and Chicago. Its classical musicians are superb; Lois Marshall and Glenn Gould are musicians of the first rank; the Toronto Symphony Orchestra is notably versatile and renowned for its sight-reading ability.

The music may be beautiful and the money welcome, but the city itself, wounded anew every day by expressway builders, is ugly where it isn't plain. A few aspects of the city are tolerable – the gardens of Forest Hill; the woods of Rosedale, where ancient three-storey houses can just be discerned behind the leaves; the Island on a summer day, from a canoe in one of the lagoons (plate 85); or the view from the Park Plaza roof (plate 83). But the greater part is a clutter of signs and wires, like Bloor Street at Bay (plate 84).

In the mind of a certain kind of citizen here (in the districts of Danforth and Rosedale), Toronto is still the capital of the British Empire. To remind them that there is no more Empire, and that anyway London was the capital, is useless; these are the people who on opening night of the movie *Mutiny on the Bounty*, during the playing of 'Rule Britannia', cheered and clapped. It is perhaps inevitable that people such as these, when they built a city, would reproduce the kind of sooty clutter they knew from London. Still, if the commercial streets are ugly, they are interesting and cosmopolitan. This is as yet expressed in some rather ridiculous ways – Torontonians still think, for instance, that their crowded subways (like London's) and their hellish new expressways (like New York's) make them part of the great world. Most of them still don't know or care about the great classical music being played here, or about the artists (Coughtry, Snow, Nakamura, *et al.*) working here. Ballet (the National Ballet at rehearsal, plate 81), opera, and dramatic theatre have not prospered with orchestral music except in that offshoot of Toronto – Stratford. They are, however, increasingly popular as the post-war European immigrants who make up almost half the city come to the theatres for their Verdi, Fry, or Tchaikovsky.

At the St Lawrence Market and directly under the feet of the dancers (plate 81) are the storekeepers and the farmers (plate 82), including some Mennonites from round the city, who every Saturday sell fresh vegetables and such country treasures as locust honey and fresh lake trout.

Just beyond the skyline of the down-town city (plate 83) runs the line of Toronto Island (upper right). Here the city is creating a peaceful park, and here its yacht clubs are based. Most of the boats are sailing sloops, but some power boats and canoes use the lagoons among the islands (plate 85). This picture, taken in late October when the weather was still hot and roses were still blooming, catches an aspect of the city almost unknown to other Canadians. Part of the climatological-botanical region known as the Carolinian forest zone (plates 83–104), the Toronto area has many indigenous species of plant usually associated with the sub-tropics; it is so mild in the city that flowers (the Christmas rose, and the hyacinth) have bloomed outdoors in every month except January.

Sailors at the Island yacht clubs, disregarding the soot that stains their sails and the polluted water corroding their hulls, make their boats ready for a Saturday sail. Dragon sailors from Toronto's waterfront yacht clubs have repeatedly won world prizes, beating English, Norwegians, Danes, Americans. Toronto's pre-eminence in International 14s, regarded by most sailors as the most difficult sailing, is so pronounced now that their chief competitors – Americans, Bermudans, and Englishmen – come here to study the new Canadian hulls and watch training programmes and racing techniques, for copying at home.

Beyond the sailboats, the new docks of Toronto Harbour reach into the filthy water, loaded with imports of Volkswagens, wheat, sugar, exports of Fords, tractors, aircraft. Although the harbour is probably the best on the lakes, the traffic has not multiplied as quickly as expected since the Seaway was opened. (Yearly tonnage has levelled off at just under 5,000,000.) Yet the city has grown phenomenally, in people and in business. The population, at 1,950,000, is triple the 1945 total, and the city by most of the commercial yardsticks is now richer and stronger – and perhaps uglier – than any other city in Canada.

86–87, NIAGARA FALLS is, in strictly physical terms, a
90–96 limestone ledge with fresh water falling over it. To most Canadians who live in its fall-out range, Niagara is the magnification of a cliché, although it may well provide their way of life, through its tourist industry or electricity. Yet in the very magnification, the falls are unique. The spray and pound of the falling water is oceanic; the frozen floes (plate 86, left) crouched over the fall's edge are like Labrador icebergs. The distance from shore to shore is 1,000 feet, the height of the falls 167 feet, the hydro-electric development on the Canadian side alone over 2,000,000 horsepower.

The ways that Canadians have devised to provide views of the falls are so numerous and various that they are funny: there is a pair of little boats, each named *Maid of the Mist*, that bob around in the Whirlpool Rapids right under the falls; you can take the Scenic Tunnel trip, dressed in slicker and rain-hat, down through the rock to the Observation Plaza, and stare powerlessly at the water bursting out of the river above your head; you can cross to the United States on an aerial buggy suspended on cables above the gyrating water of the Whirlpool Rapids; you can walk to the States on the little wooden footbridge spanning the river at the Whirlpool Rapids. You can fly over the falls in a little plane, or in a helicopter; you can go up a tower 325 feet high overlooking the falls, or like some of the local daredevils you could get into the traditional barrel and fall over the falls. Even barrels may go out of style: in 1961, Roger Woodward, aged seven years, wearing a life-jacket, fell into the river and was swept over the Horseshoe Falls. He was picked up in the whirlpool below, alive and well.

The water cascading over the Horseshoe Falls (plate 87, seen from the Seagram Tower) is of basic importance to one of the richest, most bountiful parts of Canada, a long peninsula of land jutting west from the line Toronto–Midland. Lake Ontario, Lake Erie, Lake Huron, Georgian Bay, and Lake Simcoe surround this section of low hills and fertile plateaux, making it almost an island, keeping it mild in winter, relatively cool in summer, and moist through the long growing season (at Windsor, 220 days). West from Toronto to Sarnia runs a climatic-botanical line of immense importance to the whole nation, the line that divides the typical Canadian mixed forest zone, to the north, from a peculiar area called the Carolinian zone. In this large zone (approximately 22,000 square miles – twice the size of Belgium) many of the indigenous plants and trees are sub-tropical. The Carolinian zone, which extends through Mississippi into Louisiana, is named from the Carolinas of the United States, where it is best developed. In Carolinian Ontario, the indigenous herbaceous plants include the Lotus flower, May apple, wild yam vine, prickly pear, and ginseng. The trees include sassafras, paw-paw, sycamore, magnolia, Kentucky coffee, and red bud or Judas tree. These are the ornaments of a climate that supports orchards of apricots, pears, peaches, and apples, vineyards of wine and table grapes, fields that yield two or three fodder crops in a year and, formerly, big groves of hardwoods (black walnut, curly maple, black cherry) which the pioneers of the nineteenth century converted into magnificent furniture. The men who opened this land to cultivation found huge flocks of wild turkeys, which were common in the eastern and southern States but unknown elsewhere in Canada.

The frost-free season at Point Pelee averages 197 days, only two weeks shorter than Vancouver's, and three weeks longer than Penticton's, in the fruitful Okanagan Valley of southern British Columbia. The waters draining away through Niagara help to keep this climate mild, for, when the cold fronts sag south over the continent in the winter, they come from the north-west and must pass over Superior, Michigan, Huron, and Georgian Bay to reach this land, and they are warmed in the passing. The influence of Lakes Ontario and Erie spreads north miles inland, keeping frosts short and shallow.

A little north of the richest belt, the country rises through a plateau into rolling hills, and there the climate is sterner. Yet the Scots, German, and Loyalist pioneers clearing the land found it fertile and built their rail fences (plate 95) round fields that produced wheat bountifully. The stook of wheat or other grain (plates 92-4, 96) is not so common, now that the great combines have invaded Ontario fields. These fields produced more wheat than any other area in Canada up to about 1915, when the West overtook them. Old methods have lingered longer here than on the great spreads of Saskatchewan (plate 92, forking up stooks by hand). The farms helped to create an industry in farm machinery that grew up behind tariff walls, then branched out successfully to Europe, South America, and Asia. The horse-drawn Massey-Harris reapers, binders, thrashing machines, rakes (plate 93) are cast aside now, and the sub-marginal land, too, has been given to secondary uses such as growing Scotch pines for Christmas-trees (plate 91).

88-89 The people of STRATFORD, Ontario, used to their Romeo and Juliet streets, their River Avon, and Gad's Hill, decided impetuously in 1953 to give to their 'airy nothing a local habitation and a name'. Prompted by a local dreamer named Tom Patterson, they

called in Alec Guinness, Tyrone Guthrie, Tanya Moiseiwitsch, and a tent-maker to make them a Shakespearean Festival. Now, the Festival is housed in a magnificent theatre built round the original stage (plate 89) designed for the first tent theatre by Tanya Moiseiwitsch. It has presented Shakespearean comedies, histories, and tragedies, but has ventured further, with *Oedipus Rex*, *Cyrano de Bergerac*, original Canadian plays, light opera, Bach concerts, film and book festivals, and touring companies that have played Shaw and Marlowe in high-school auditoriums in Canada and great theatres in New York.

Many Canadian players have gone from Stratford to Broadway or the West End, including Frances Hyland, Christopher Plummer, and Kate Reid. Irene Worth, Alec Guinness, and Siobhan McKenna have acted here, and great Canadian musicians have given concerts on this stage, among them Glenn Gould and Lois Marshall. From the start, Stratford has been first class, and today's companies are still developing fine new talents. Martha Henry as Cressida rehearses *Troilus and Cressida* (plate 88) with Douglas Rain (Ulysses), Peter Donat (Troilus, background), and Len Birman (Diomedes).

Garrick Hagon (Patroclus; under stage balcony, plate 89), Leo Ciceri (Achilles; cloaked, centre stage), John Colicos (Hector; in cape, facing Ciceri), and Peter Donat (helmet, front of group on right side) rehearse *Troilus and Cressida*, which was designed by Desmond Heeley, directed by Michael Langham, and presented in 1963.

97-100 Along the southern edge of Georgian Bay (near COLLINGWOOD, plate 97) is a region of high hills loaded with snow almost four months of the year, and supporting medium-length ski runs (maximum vertical drop: 800 feet). The orchards from Collingwood (plate 98) to Owen Sound are all apples: stone fruits will not thrive this far north, although grapes do, wild and cultivated.

A March day in the woods here can be beautiful beyond imagination (plate 97). Following the steaming horses round the woods gathering maple syrup, while the sun shines and the creeks begin to run, you feel the strength of the sun reawakening life, in the blood, in the sap of the trees pinging into the steel

pails. Lampman expressed such a day in his poem
'Winter-Break':

> All day between high-curded clouds the sun
> Shone down like summer on the steaming planks.
> The long bright icicles in dwindling ranks
> Dripped from the murmuring eaves till one by one
> They fell. As if the spring had now begun,
> The quilted snow, sun-softened to the core,
> Loosened and shunted with a sudden roar
> From downward roofs.

101-2 To catch a whitefish, view the day, or shovel snow
from a threatened summer cottage roof, men walk out
on the ice of GEORGIAN BAY (near Parry Sound,
plate 102) which at mid-winter is often frozen to a
depth of four feet. Where the snow does not cover it,
the hard blue ice has a beauty of its own: when pressure cracks appear (plate 101) in transparent fields, or
on a day when the whole lake, though frozen, appears
quite open. This happens when a thaw sets in after an
early freeze, and the ice melts into little white balls,
rounded by wave action. Then on a still, cold night
the lake re-freezes, the ice between the white balls dark
and clear, so that the balls appear still to be floating on
the surface, though in fact the ice is six inches thick
around them.

A peculiar vehicle has been invented to traverse this
ice. It is called a scoot, and it is about fifteen to twenty
feet long, with a metal, toboggan-shaped bottom, and
an aeroplane engine and a propeller caged on top of
the rear section with an air rudder behind. The faster
scoots can do up to about 100 m.p.h. over ice. Carrying two to four people in a cabin, they can cross slush,
open water, ice-floes mixed in water, sheer ice, and
snowed ice. They are invaluable among the cloud of
islands along the east coast of Georgian Bay, for without them the Indians and white cottagers could not
travel during six to ten weeks of winter.

103-5 Like a huge limestone dock jutting out between
Georgian Bay and Lake Huron, the BRUCE
PENINSULA stretches north-west, covered with
tourists and farmers (plate 105). The Bruce supports
wild flowers rare in Canada, including the hart's-
tongue fern and many varieties of orchid, among them
the Alaska. So precious are the flowers that the
Ontario government posts stern signs warning everyone not to pick them. No part of the Bruce is more
than ten miles from the lake, hence the seagulls by the
tractor (plate 105).

Farther north, on MANITOULIN ISLAND, the
same limestone recurs (plate 103). The people here are
quiet, and proud that it is from 'The Manitoulin', as
they call it, that Lester Pearson has gone to win the
Nobel Peace Prize, and to lead Canada and the
Liberal Party. Progress has been missing here: today
the people farm almost as they did one hundred years
ago, when the island was settled. They still use the
squared-log barns (plate 104), and the snake fences
here are not only being renewed, but built new –
probably the only place in Ontario apart from Upper
Canada Village where this is true on a mass scale.
Tractors are not new here but about one-third of the
farmers don't have one: they plough behind horses.
Nearly all the other farmers keep horses, too, because
they go through the island's deep winter drifts when
tractors fail.

106-7 This is the SHIELD (variously named pre-Cambrian,
Laurentian, and Canadian), which formerly was so
important to Canadian life that the whole nation was
shaped and nourished by it. Its furs, forests, and waters
were the nation. Almost the only, and certainly the
earliest, parts of Canada explored and settled by
Europeans were in the Shield, or dependent on it for
trade goods. The country still depends on the woods
for paper (Canada produces forty-five per cent of the
world newsprint total, and paper pays more wages in
total than any other industry in Canada), on the rocks
for minerals (asbestos, iron, nickel), and on the rivers
for hydro-electricity. But few people live in the old
north now: from being a relatively populous and
civilized part of the country, it has changed to the
emptiest and most primitive.

The hemlock in the foreground are typical of the
great forests stretching north from this Superior shore
(at Superior Provincial Park, plate 106; near
Marathon, plate 107). Mixed with them grow birch,
pine, black spruce, tamarack – all useful for newsprint, furniture, or plywood.

To travel by canoe through such country is to leave
the modern world for something so different that com-

parisons do not exist. The engine is muscle, the shelter canvas, the food dehydrated or fresh killed, and the scenery beyond criticism. Even at its most dangerous or difficult, this shining country is beautiful; the rocks in the rapids shine red and gold in the spray; the uphill portage trail smells sweetly of balsam; the cry of the loon before rain is so poignant it seems almost holy. Lonely it is, but not unfriendly if you know how to use it, and certainly the people, no matter how remote they are geographically, warm you like a winter fire.

This rim of Lake Superior has only recently been opened to automobiles, with the completion of the Trans-Canada Highway. The highest point in a flat province (2,120 feet, at Tip Top Hill) stands behind these hills (plate 106) south of Superior Provincial Park.

108-9 For a Westerner coming down from Calgary to the prairies, for an Easterner coming to this WINNIPEG on the banks of the Red River, the first sight of these plains is an appalling experience. The immensity of the sky, the flatness of the land, the lack of feature and variation, are enough to make a stranger pity the people who live here, and to send him home as fast as he can go. But for the plainsman born, the shadow forms of the clouds moving immensely over the land, the sight of thunderheads a hundred miles away on the horizon bar, the feeling that your shoulders are level with eternity – these are enough to dismiss mere valleys or shores as possible homes. W.O. Mitchell has described his prairie in the opening chapter of his novel *Who Has Seen the Wind*: '. . . prairie lay wide around the town, stretching tan to the far line of the sky, shimmering under the June sun and waiting for the unfailing visitation of wind, gentle at first, barely stroking the long grasses. . . . Where the snow-white of alkali edged the course of the river, a thin trickle of water made its way toward the town low upon the horizon. Silver willow, heavy with dust, grew along the riverbanks, perfuming the air with its honey smell.'

The river and Winnipeg are inseparable. The Red and the Assiniboine supported the first settlements, and now, running through the city's centre, they are lined with docks and boathouses where people keep big cruisers, outboards, rowboats, and canoes, which they can use to travel miles up or down either river, and into Lake Winnipeg.

It is true that, to the traveller arriving from the east, Winnipeg, netted in poles and wires, looms on the horizon like a disaster, but there is nothing average or ugly about the life of the people here. The city has been from its foundation one of the most interesting in Canada. From the great bubble-time wittily described in Stephen Leacock's reminiscence of his Uncle Bill, when fortunes floated up and down Portage Avenue waiting for men to snatch them out of the air, through the riotous twenties and thirties, the city has always been intense and varied. It has probably more significant minorities than even Montreal: here, Scots, Icelanders, Mennonites, Ukrainians, English, French, Métis (or half-breeds), Jews and Christians from Russia, Poland, and Germany, and lately Americans, have come in and made a babel, usually joyful, and sometimes not.

Rivers and railways as well as races meet here. The Assiniboine (plate 108, left) joins the Red River (plate 108, right) to flow through Lake Winnipeg, then on to Hudson Bay. The C.N.R. and the C.P.R. have their great western marshalling-yards here, routing grain down to the Lakehead at Port Arthur–Fort William. The members of the provincial legislature meet here (Legislative Building, plate 109, lower right). And at Winnipeg meet two extremes of weather – Arctic cold and desert heat – sometimes so abruptly in spring that the rivers, unable to carry the resulting run-off, inundate the city. In 1950 was the worst recent example: after a cold spring, following a winter in which prairie temperatures averaged twenty-five degrees below their normal, a sudden thaw combined with heavy precipitation flooded the city and drove thousands of people from their homes. The January isotherm (line of mean temperature for an area), which runs by Winnipeg, stretches through the Arctic to the Pole. It is the coldest major city in Canada. The January mean is zero, and it has been as low as fifty-four below in the city. The winter temperature often stays at zero or less for four to six weeks. Yet in July the heat has been as high as a hundred and eight degrees, and temperatures of a hundred or more have been recorded in every month from May to the end of September.

Now under construction, and due to be completed

in 1968, is a tremendous flood-control system, which was expected at the outset to cost $85 million. The most important part will be a floodway thirty miles long skirting the east end of Winnipeg, to carry off excess waters of the Red River. There will also be a dam and a diversion system to the west.

When Rupert Brooke visited the city in 1913, he found that it had more promise for the future than any of the other Canadian cities he had visited, because it had broken away from the prevailing mores of North America and was on its way to a destiny different from any other city's. That he was prescient has been proven amply. The Winnipeg General Strike after the war, the continuous strength of Socialism, the strength, beauty, and originality of the Royal Winnipeg Ballet, of the various dramatic groups, and of its writers (Gabrielle Roy, Jack Ludwig, Adele Wiseman) have proved that the city has a kind of progressive drive lacking in the east, not likely to slow even under the weight of its present affluence.

110–18 Lemoine Fitzgerald, the Group of Seven painter, used to lie on his back and sketch the clouds over southern Manitoba, and Peter Varley has found the same fascination in the ranked clouds over the eastern approach to REGINA, Saskatchewan (plate 110). In the foreground is the Trans-Canada Highway, here four lanes wide, and, all round the city, farming country.

SASKATCHEWAN is a big farm, supporting 627,000 rural people, 129,000 more than live in its urban areas. In only three other provinces do the rural people now outnumber the urban. Running against the Canadian population trend, Saskatchewan declined in numbers of people between 1931 and 1941 (2.8 per cent), and 1941 and 1951 (7.2 per cent). Partly, this was because of the urban drift – farm-boys going to the cities to find jobs. But it was due as well to the dustbowl conditions that prevailed here in the droughted thirties, when, during the time of Prime Minister Bennett, farming was so unproductive that the farmers could not afford gas for their new Model T Fords and hitched them to horses – hence 'Bennett buggies'. The province has begun to grow again, but its rate is still the slowest in Canada. Unless new farming techniques open the thinly settled lakeland to the north, it is not likely to grow quickly. It is pros-

perous now: the 95,000 operating farmers shared $630 million net in 1963, an average of $6,750. The average for 1961, a drought year, was $1,475, and the average for the 1950s was about $3,400.

The agricultural future in Saskatchewan seems to lie in water control. The South Saskatchewan River Dam Project, now well under way, is due to irrigate half a million acres of land. By March 1961, fifty-four irrigation projects affecting a further half-million acres had been begun. There were 461 drainage and flood-control projects under way, and topographic surveys had been carried out on 200,000 acres. In a land so flat that a tussock six feet high is a geographical feature, creeks, dikes, dams, and irrigation canals mean the difference between Libyan desert and fertile grassland or farms. People through the West are well aware that Libya was once a fertile province of the Roman Empire.

The North Saskatchewan, which flows through a remarkably deep trench (seen here at Edmonton, looking north past the high-level auto and C.P.R. bridge towards the Provincial Government Buildings, plate 111) keeps its peace more than the Red. The river here is 140 feet wide, and the valley in which it runs is 100 feet deep, in places deeper. (Down-stream to the Forks the banks average between 200 and 300 feet.) Calgary, which stands beside part of the south branch (here called the Bow) 175 miles south-west of Edmonton, is 3,540 feet above sea-level and thus 2,830 feet above the mouth of the Saskatchewan itself, where it empties into Lake Winnipeg. This drop is spread over a meandering run of about 800 miles. Where the rivers are trenched deep, and irrigation does not reach, the prairies are desert-dry as in southern Alberta – cactus country (plate 118). This common cactus (*Opuntia polyacantha*) is widespread in certain parts of southern British Columbia and Alberta, parts commonly known as dry-belt, where the average annual rainfall is less than ten inches. This total seems more than it is: much of it falls in summer, and is immediately drawn off the land by dry winds and hot sunshine. The low rainfall, though not the desert flora, extends far into South-Central Saskatchewan (around Moose Jaw, plate 112). The change in flora may be due to the colder winters in Saskatchewan, where the effects of the chinook (warm winter winds) are not so strong.

Disastrous to farmers, the effects of erosion are picturesque in the Badlands (plate 115) around Drumheller in the Red Deer River valley, seventy-five miles west of Calgary. Here, in dry, white-grey soil, dinosaur bones and tropical fossils are constantly being found. For a while Drumheller district did a remarkable export business in dinosaur bones: museums in eastern Canada, the United States, and Europe collected fairly complete skeletons, by now numbering over thirty.

Mr Varley has created (plate 115) an effect reminiscent of the huge Early Egyptian temples and statues carved into rock on the Nile near Aswan, but the scale here is miniature: the area shown in the photograph measures about 6 feet high by 9 feet wide.

The prairies have accommodated, besides 'Bennett buggies', all kinds of odd transport, including railways that run straight as a ruled line for scores of miles (plates 113, 114). The Indians first went on foot; then, after the wild Spanish horses drifted north, they tamed the colts and invented the travois, a V of springy poles dragged behind the ponies, to carry children or goods. White men came up-river in *canots du nord*, light birch canoes, then in steamboats, once common and essential on the Saskatchewan. They accomplished the opening of the West in the high-wheeled, squealing Red River carts that went west from Fort Garry, shrieking like guinea-hens. The latest attack on distance is the pipeline: it exports both gas and oil from Alberta to eastern Canada, and technicians in Edmonton are now experimenting with a new type that will move solids suspended in a moving mass of fluid.

The mountain alder (plates 116, 117) is in North America a typically Western tree, growing in Canada from the mouth of the Mackenzie south to the border, and west from Central Saskatchewan to the Pacific. It usually grows alone in unmixed stands that have a crinkled appearance, because the trunks are both light barked and crooked. The leaves (plate 117) are coarse and hairy.

119-28   The eastern foothills of the Rocky Mountains are among the loveliest regions of Canada. The prairie, which has been rising almost imperceptibly in shallow steps towards Calgary (plate 119), here breaks up into tremendous ranges, not quite mountains but hinting at the sea of mountains beyond, no longer prairie but fertile as the blackest of Manitoba land. In the south, the main streams, many flowing from the Columbia Glacier high in the Rockies, are tributaries of the Saskatchewan. In the Peace River country to the north, the land is watered by the Peace, flowing from its sources in the Rocky Mountain Trench to the Arctic. Among these hills, the towns, such as High River, begin to feel the effects of the Pacific on trade (plate 121) and on climate. Although Calgary is 3,500 feet above sea-level, it is much warmer through winter than lower prairie cities, because the hot chinook winds keep the atmosphere dry, clear, and warm. The chinooks originate in the Pacific, when warm wet air rises slowly up the west flank of the mountains, cooling as it expands at the higher altitudes, and losing its moisture. When it flows down the east side of the mountains, it warms up again by compression at the lower altitudes. The warming rate of the dried air is twice the cooling rate of the ascending wet air. The chinook effect is most dramatic on a cold January day: there is a hesitant feeling in the atmosphere – suddenly the bright western air, a sharp line against the polar clouds, shoves the clouds to the east, the temperature leaps up as much as sixty degrees in a couple of hours, and the snow on the ground vanishes without a trace. The chinook helps to keep the average Calgary January mean at a tolerable fifteen degrees, while Winnipeg (zero) and Edmonton (seven degrees) suffer.

The sense of space, of plentiful land and air for every human being, which Indian tribes east and west seem to have shared, still exists among the Indians of the Stony Reserve in the foothills of Alberta (plate 120). Though of different linguistic background, the Stony Reserve Indians, like the Cree-Iroquoian of Christian Island, Georgian Bay, have set their houses much farther apart than white men would. The southern part of the reserve, south of the Bow River, has recently been opened by the Trans-Canada Highway section running to Banff.

The saddle horses (also called ponies, Indian ponies, and pintos, plates 122, 125) of the West are still used for rounding up cattle, or for riding for pleasure through the foothills country. A man may saddle up at his own barn at dawn, with his son, carrying fishing-rods, and ride to a trout pool on a river such as the Highwood (here seen twenty-five miles west of High River, Alberta, plate 123), and pull out half a dozen brook trout for breakfast; here, the Highwood is still a clear mountain stream. He will spend the rest of the day in a valley such as this one (plate 124) south of the Highwood and east of Mount Burke, 8,360 feet, where his cattle have excellent grass-land. His business is done in a little town such as Pincher Creek (population 2,961), only a few miles from the first abrupt surge of the mountains (plate 126, looking south towards Victoria Peak, 8,460 feet, and Mount Haig, 8,565). Willow Valley (plate 128) is in the southern foothills, shaded from the west by the eastern ridge of the Rockies, which separate it from the Kananaskis River valley on the far side.

From Cowley, Alberta, near the United States border, Highway 3 runs towards Crow's Nest Pass in the southern Rockies. Here the mountains rise very steeply from relatively level plateau land. Crow's Nest Mountain is 9,138 feet high, and the prevailing heights are 8,000 to 9,000 feet. Near here occurred in 1903 the famous Frank Slide: after a short earth-tremor, about 90 million tons of rock fell from Turtle Mountain on the town of Frank in the Crow's Nest Pass. Sixty-six people died under the rock. Although the slide was later estimated to have lasted only two minutes, perhaps less, it covered a square mile of the valley to a depth of forty-five feet. Marks of smaller slides are visible in many of the mountain illustrations (including plate 128, centre and left).

The fences along Highway 3 (plate 127) are permanent snow fences. Annual snowfall in this area is about eighty inches, drifted over the highways by the prevailing south-west wind.

129–34 Yellowknife (plate 129), NORTHWEST TERRI-TORIES, on the north shore of Great Slave Lake (sixty-two degrees N.) is at roughly the same latitude as Bergen, Norway, where rhododendrons grow wild, but the Canadian town is in the forest and barrens region of Canada, sub-Arctic in climate, and only 200 or so miles from the tree-line (beyond which trees cannot grow). The January mean daily temperature, fourteen below zero, is bitter, but humidity is rela-

tively low and the winds are light. The growing season is long for the Canadian inland region – both July and August are frost-free in the average year, and there is usually only one night in June with frost. (Whitehorse, nearer the Pacific, farther south, and generally warmer, nevertheless has more summer frost because it is higher – 2,289 feet to Yellowknife's 682.)

First settled in 1934 during a gold rush, Yellow-knife was largely deserted until 1944, when the rush resumed. The population now is 3,200, up from 2,700 in 1951, and the town is an important way-point on routes to the Far North.

Two places on the Coppermine River, 400 air-miles to the north, have been served by Yellowknife. Sixty miles from the river-mouth town and well beyond the tree-line, Canadian scientists at Speers Lake worked on the Upper Mantle Project in 1963, probing with hard-rock drilling equipment (flown up from North Bay, Ontario, via Yellowknife) a mile into the earth's upper mantle (the layer immediately below the earth's crust) to discover its composition and characteristics. A preliminary discovery was that the permafrost, or permanently frozen layer of surface earth, was about 700 feet deep in this area.

On the Coppermine River, just south of the Dismal Lakes, the upper mantle appears in a fault at the sur-face of the earth – a rare occurrence. Fuel for running the drills (plate 130), flown up in steel drums, is stored outdoors. After use, the drums, worth nine dollars each, are abandoned, because to fly them back would be too expensive.

In May, when the snow pictures were taken (plates 132, 134) by Toronto photographer Herbert Taylor, the sun was strong, and had pocked the snow during the day, converting the solid to a vapour in the dry air without any melting stage (at air temperatures around zero to twenty-five degrees).

Isachsen (plates 131, 133) on Ellef Ringnes Island (seventy-nine degrees N.) is one of the Far North's remotest settlements. Primarily a weather station, operated jointly by Canada and the United States, Isachsen is also used as an exploration base for the Federal government's Polar Continental Shelf Project, accommodating up to seventy or eighty scientists and technicians who are doing a dozen different kinds of survey and research work in the Arctic islands.

Primitive and modern methods combine oddly: the helicopter (plate 131) flew out over the ocean and landed on the ice, where the scientists chopped a hole in the ice and lowered a hand-line to find the depth and get a sample of the ocean floor. Standing on the airstrip (plate 133), one of the pilots measures the wind velocity with a hand anemometer before take-off.

135-7 DAWSON is a hung-over town, from the gold rush of the nineties, and now from the festival there in 1962, when stars imported from Broadway (Bert Lahr) and from Toronto (Pierre Berton), and crowds of tourists gave it again some of the old glamour and beat. Inspired by the same Tom Patterson who revivified Stratford, Ontario, the Dawson Festival was supposed to attract hordes of tourists up the Alaska Highway. The festival was sponsored by the Federal, territorial, and municipal governments, and thus got off to a good financial start. However, the 20,000 tourists who came didn't spend enough, and the deficit of $396,000 has been a comic point in debates in the House of Commons off and on since then.

There were moments during the festival when it seemed Dawson might be on the rebound, moments like those when Black Mike Winage (plate 136), dressed up for the occasion, leaned out of the royal box at the Palace Grand Theatre and started to shout jokes at Bert Lahr during the world première of the musical *Foxy* by Ring Lardner, Jr., and Ian M. Hunter. Black Mike, born in Serbia, has been in Dawson since about 1898, when he came up to mine gold. In his nineties now, he still has a strong voice, his health, and a position as foreman of the Dawson Street Department.

Viewed from a side-hill near Suicide Point, on the trail to the Indian village of Moosehide, some of Black Mike's Dawson streets run along the river-front just above the point where the Klondike River (left) enters the Yukon (plate 137). During gold-rush days the home of about 25,000 people, Dawson has a population of about 850 today.

A couple of miles up-river from Dawson is the Indian settlement of Moosehide, where the Horst Scheffer family lives (plate 135). Descendants of a German settler who married a Loucheux Indian woman, the Scheffers live in a log cabin (30 feet by

15 feet) faced near the entrance with boards. The typical occupations of the settlement are trapping in winter, and fishing or hunting in summer. Close to the river, the settlement is connected to Dawson only by a rough trail in off-season or by the river in winter and summer. There are no streets at Moosehide, but trails from one house to another, with wide spaces separating the houses. A school building stands on the settlement's grounds, but there is no teacher. A portrait of Queen Elizabeth on the schoolhouse wall has been shot by a rifle bullet, and some of the windows are broken.

138-43 Last in the tremendous geographical experiences of Canadians – the Great River, the Great Lakes, the Great Plains, the ROCKIES – these mountains have been pierced but not civilized. Edward Blake, the Liberal leader opposing the Confederation railway schemes of the 1870s, told the House of Commons at Ottawa that at that time it was madness to try to build a railway 'through that sea of mountains'. The nation disagreed, and in July 1886 Prime Minister John A. Macdonald with his wife, Susan Agnes, was riding the cow-catcher of a C.P.R. locomotive as it headed west, sometimes straight through the mountains – the Connaught Tunnel in the Selkirk Range is five miles long.

The triviality of what men do is nowhere in Canada so apparent as here: not only may the railways or highways be destroyed in a moment by millions of tons of rock washing them away like water melting sand, but, even where the mountains do not threaten physically, they amuse by the scale they set against our cabins and bridges. A trapper's cabin seven feet high is built alone on a mountain standing 12,000 feet high; on a valley fence encircling a peak a sign reads 'Private Property' and you look up to the peak 13,000 feet high, its tip creating private clouds.

If in North America these mountains are big, they are tremendous by European standards: in height the Alps range down from Mont Blanc (15,782 feet), and they extend to the east a few hundred miles and are only a few score miles across. The North American Cordillera runs for thousands of miles from north to south; the Rocky chain alone reaches a width of a hundred miles, and is only one of three main chains which together are 600 miles wide in many places, from foothills to mountainous sea-coast. The highest of the Canadian mountains, Mount Logan, in the St Elias Range, Yukon, is 4,000 feet higher than Mont Blanc. Norwegians who have ridden the famous Bergen–Oslo railway come back from the C.P.R. or the C.N.R. lines in British Columbia saying that their own line is small stuff compared with the Canadian ones; but, more surprisingly, they come back in awe from their visits to the fjords of British Columbia, stunned to realize that their own fjords are so small, so short, by comparison.

After the great railway-building, when the mountains were first pierced by permanent forms of transportation (the fur-traders were the first to cross by foot and canoe, ahead of even the Indians), there was a lag in the attack on the valleys. A few roads were built; Trans-Canada Air Lines opened its first trans-mountain passenger service in March 1938 with Lockheed 10 aircraft. Now, the Trans-Canada Highway, recently completed, crosses the Rocky Range between Lake Louise and the Golden–Donald Station road, where it turns west, following much the same country as the C.P.R. line, but opening for the first time to automobile traffic the spectacular country from Rogers Pass (named after Major A. B. Rogers, who explored it for the C.P.R. in 1881) down to Glacier. This straight-line cut-off saves motorists the 170-mile loop trip over a poor road from Donald to Revelstoke. The country through which tourists may now drive on a modern, long-curved, shallow-grade highway is typified by the photographs of the Rockies (in the Kananaskis River country, plate 138; at Peyto Lake, twenty-six miles north of Banff, plate 139), and of the Selkirks (plate 143). After he crosses the Rockies, the tourist runs fourteen miles up the Rocky Mountain Trench from Golden to Donald Station, then turns in towards Rogers Pass. Before the builder's scars healed, he could look straight into the darkness of the full evergreen forest, without the impediment of underbrush (plate 140). On the eastern slope of Mount Tupper (9,239 feet), near Glacier, he will see this C.P.R. bridge (plate 141) joining two mountains, and all around will be mountains such as these (plates 142, 143) in the Hermit Range, which averages 8,000 to 10,000 feet above sea-level. The Western white

spruce (plate 142, left) is common in this area, with lodgepole pine, Engelmann spruce, Rocky Mountain fir, and Douglas fir. In this latitude, the spruce grow at altitudes of 3,000 to 6,000 feet, neatly marking off for the practised eye the heights of all the mountains in sight.

144 Steamboats in the mountains, and railways were REVELSTOKE's making. Now the town, 379 miles north-east of Vancouver, at the western edge of the Rockies, is on the Trans-Canada Highway, and tourism is overtaking railways in its life. The surrounding farmland (plate 144) on the plateau about 1,500 feet above sea-level is ringed with mountains rising to 11,000 feet. The 'turret' appearing at top right is actually part of a long ridge neatly cut off by cloud cover. The ridge is covered with snow (the photographs were taken in June) and the speckles are trees. The higher mountains (above 6,000 feet) even in southern British Columbia are snow-covered all year, and thus are a constant source of water for the mountain streams, a vital consideration to farms south and west of here, where the rainfall averages ten inches or less per year. Immediately round Revelstoke, and all down the west flank of the Selkirks, however, the rain situation is much better: the photograph has caught the kind of light cloud cover that constantly forms on these mountain slopes and makes the west Selkirk flank the wettest part of the British Columbia interior. The extreme of this weather situation is reached at Glacier (4,094 feet), a few miles beyond the mountain, where the average winter snowfall is 342 inches.

145-7 In the spring of 1807, while the snow was still deep on the Rocky Mountains, David Thompson left the North Saskatchewan River with ten pack horses and headed west. He came to a place where 'mountain connected to mountain by immense glaciers, the collection of ages'. He crossed to a fast stream flowing north, later named the Columbia, and then turned south. (Thompson's description, from his narrative, is quoted in *British Columbia: a History*, by Margaret A. Ormsby.) He reached a long lake amid mountains and built Kootenae House there, the first trading-post on the Columbia River basin. In this marvellous long valley today are grassland (plates 145, 146), mines, farms, towns, and fading mementoes of the earliest days (plate 147, the church at FORT STEELE).

Thompson looked for furs, among other things, and the ensuing trade of the North West Company in the area bore out his faith in building Kootenae House. After the Nor' Wester era came government, with the establishment of a North West Mounted Police post at Fort Steele in 1887. This was the first N.W.M.P. fort in British Columbia. The church attached to the fort still stands, though disused (plate 147).

The steep nature of the Rocky Mountain Trench, down whose east flank Thompson descended, is clear here in the shot taken across grassland looking towards Fernie (plate 145). The mountains here range from 7,000 to 9,000 feet, and Crow's Nest Pass, through them, is 4,500 feet.

Where the clouds touch the grass, at altitudes between 1,500 and 3,500 feet along the southern slopes of these hills, grows the Ponderosa pine (plates 145, 146). Common in the western United States, the Ponderosa – orange-barked, deeply cleft when old, and tall (160–80 feet) – grows from the southern Rockies west almost to the Fraser at about Lillooet, but not on the coast. The broken twigs have a light, sharp smell like crushed orange-peel.

148–51 'This whole area is lifted into a lighter, paler feeling than I have ever experienced before', wrote Peter Varley after photographing the country round the KOOTE-NAY LAKES. 'All the colour tones are lighter, the water is pale green, even the evergreens seem lighter. The textures of things here are rough (except for the wave-washed pebbles, plate 150): the rocks, the Ponderosa pine-bark – even the weather. This lake has amazingly quick storms.' Part of the reason for this is the character of the lake and the shore. Although Kootenay Lake is over sixty miles long, its area is only 168 square miles, and the mountains at each side rise abruptly to 7,000–8,000 feet, which is 5,500 to 6,500 feet above the lake level (see plate 151, the steep shore at the narrows near Balfour).

In the past, the mountain walls echoed with the sound of steam-whistles as paddle-wheelers took supplies in from the north end of the Arrow Lakes-Kootenay system; now the boats are modern ferries, carrying cars (plate 151, near Nelson) and sport-

fishing boats (plate 149), built for rod-fishing such game fish as Kamloops cut-throat, Kokanee and Dolly Varden trout, and large-mouthed bass. Fishing here and in the Okanagan lasts from April to November. Kootenay and Okanagan lakes rarely freeze over.

Wrinkled and twisted like driftwood, the mountainous west shore of the lake (seen from Boswell on the east side, three miles across, plate 148) rises steeply to Ymir Mountain (7,920 feet), seven miles inland. The C.P.R.'s Kettle Valley-Crow's Nest line runs along the west lakeshore.

152–3 The misapprehension of Canada as a cold country is exposed in the DRY-BELT REGION of southern British Columbia (as well as on the coast and in southern Ontario), not just by dry-belt cactus and sagebrush, but by cash crops of such fruits as the Moor-park, Tilton, and Blenheim apricots, which are so tender that they scarcely ripen in England unless carefully protected and trained against a sheltering wall. But here, apricot orchards produce scores of thousands of bushels a year: the total production in Canada varies from a quarter to a third of a million bushels a year, grown here and in southern Ontario.

The dry-belt, whose south-eastern corner is at Grand Forks (plate 152), extends to the north-west as far as the Thompson River near its exit from Kamloops Lake (plate 153). Throughout most of this large area, measuring roughly 10,000 square miles, the annual precipitation is ten inches or less, and the farms, especially the orchards, depend on irrigation. All the major irrigation projects in British Columbia in 1962 were in this area (except for a few in the adjacent Columbia and Kettle River valleys, which lie in the same rain shadow, extending east from the coast range).

About 35,000 acres were irrigated under these projects, with a further 18,000 potentially irrigable. Total of lands previously irrigated in British Columbia is 218,000, again chiefly in the dry-belt. The water comes from the clear, cold mountain streams which in most cases come parallel straight down the slopes to the valley rivers, like ribs on a fishbone.

The Thompson (plate 153, near Savona) is clear and fresh, with benchlands and low side-hills covered with shimmering grasses and sagebrush. The low light of the photograph brings out the peculiar sheen of these grasses.

154-5 The excitement that grips you coming into the Upper Fraser Valley is extraordinary: everyone with a feel for land senses it. The river is huge and young and wild: in spring flood, as much water rushes through the 160-foot gap at Hell's Gate as normally flows in the mile-wide St Lawrence at Quebec. The upper river is a wild mountain stream, pitching down staircases of rock, tearing at its banks (plate 154, lower left), so swollen in spring that it appears to bulge up in the middle (plate 155). The violence of the water's rush appears impressively at the junction with the Thompson. In Hugh MacLennan's words: 'The Thompson is the Fraser's chief tributary, a major stream in its own right, and it does not so much enter the Fraser as smash its way into it like a liquid battering ram. From the bridge (at Lytton) I saw its water plunging into the Fraser . . . blue-green into the yellow froth. Then it completely disappeared. The Fraser swallows the Thompson in less than a hundred yards.' (From *Seven Rivers of Canada*.)

So loud in many places that people on shore cannot hear each other talk, the Fraser runs down its 400-mile canyon to Hope, where it widens and slows and begins to meander through a broad valley towards the sea at Vancouver. Seen near Hell's Gate thirty miles above Hope, the canyon carries on the west side (plate 155, right) the main C.P.R. transcontinental line, and on the east the Cariboo Highway and the C.N.R. line.

Viewed to the north from the place where the road between Lillooet and Pavilion leaves the Fraser Valley (plate 154), the Fraser turns between high hill-sides running up at an angle of about forty-five degrees. In the distance is the Camelsfoot Range (5,000–7,000 feet). The land is as dry as it looks, and skies as clear as these prevail in the area, which lies in the rain shadow of the Coast Range. Ashcroft, near by, gets 7.4 inches of precipitation in an average year.

156-8 The mountains round the SKEENA RIVER are, for height visible to the eye, among the most impressive in the country, for they rise sharply from about sea-level to 6,000 feet within a mile or so of the river (plate 156, near Terrace) and achieve 9,000 feet ten or fifteen miles

inland from there. The Seven Sisters Range (plate 157) is 9,140 feet high just six miles south from Woodcock on the river.

The river itself is navigable for coastal craft a hundred miles from its mouth near Prince Rupert, just south of the tip of the Alaska Panhandle.

The salmon fishing in this river, round the estuary, especially from mid-July to the end of September, is dazzling. In 1959, the world record for spring salmon was set in the estuary of the Skeena with the landing of a ninety-two-pound tyee, on a rod. This tidal slough (plate 158), near Kwinitsa, is just up-river from the estuary. The smaller coho salmon are abundant here too, and may, unlike other salmon, be fished right up the river into the spawning streams. One of those streams runs in the wooded valley just behind the frame farmhouse (plate 157) in the valley north of the Seven Sisters Mountains. The farmer can hunt for mule deer or Columbia blacktail (60,000 deer are taken in an average year in the province) or for the many upland game birds, including various grouse and ptarmigan.

159-61 This Tsimshian Indian graveyard near Hazelton is typical of many with its mixture of poles (plates 159, 160) and burial houses (plate 161). Occasionally, the houses, or carved coffins, were suspended on the arms of one of the poles.

The poles were originally carved with stone tools from cedar trunks, and used as decoration for houses or sometimes as actual supports, usually at the front, holding up floor joists. With the arrival of white men, metal tools became available and pole-carving grew more popular, reaching its peak in the 1890s, after which it began to decline. Paint was used to decorate the features, but the artistic essence of the family pole was stylized sculpture. Among the rank-conscious Tsimshian, the poles, some of them ninety feet high, also came to represent wealth and influence. New poles were dedicated at a potlatch, a marvellous ceremony in which the host achieved everlasting fame by giving away enormous quantities of blankets, slaves, furs, food, and canoes. There was an element of competition – a rival might try to achieve greater credit by giving away more; and a touch of canny investment – the rival might outdo the host by returning the gifts with interest. This ceremony, one of the important parts of West Coast Indian life, has been banned by the Canadian Government, with the result that former Indian shrines such as these have fallen into ruin.

162–6 Of these poles, Peter Varley wrote: '. . . a Tsimshian pole leans, rotting at the base. Its carving is strange and spiritual, reminiscent of Mayan culture far to the south, seemingly abstracting the qualities of its environment but having even deeper roots. The flaming suns carved by the Tsimshian are oval in outline, and are oddly negative in feeling. The pole is a symbol of creation perceived by a sensitive people tuned to their spiritual life, to the earth, and to the whole mysterious universe.'

Mungo Martin, one of the last of the Coast carvers, created this expressive pole (plate 162) in the late 1940s. It shows, from top to bottom, a raven, a killer whale, and an Indian chief. This, with the pole in plate 166, is in the Totem Park at the University of British Columbia, in Vancouver. The pole in plate 166 was carved before 1939 on the north part of the British Columbia coast; information about it is scanty because no testimony from the family that commis-sioned it exists now. This situation extends over much of Canadian Indian life, combated only by a few researchers, often private, occasionally with founda-tion or Government grants. Totem Park has been extended to include a Haida village with poles, dwelling-house, and grave house.

Typical of the environment in which these Indians lived are these plants and mosses (plates 163–5). The trailing moss (*Hypnum circinale*), and the leafy moss (*Mnium glabrescens*), both growing on the log (plate 163), are found only in humid forests of the West Coast of North America.

The moss encircling the cedar log (plate 164) is *Plagiothecium undulatum*, a West Coast moss that grows only in damp coniferous forests.

The Indian pipe (plate 165) grows on decayed vegetable matter – old stumps and rotten fallen logs – in conifer forests.

167–73 VANCOUVER is a beautiful city. The mountains, the forests, and the Gulf of Georgia surround it with a natural beauty that is visible from any part of the city. Many of the residential streets are exceptionally wide,

edged with gardens that bloom ten or eleven months of the year; the residential architecture is the most advanced of any large city in Canada; the sea air blows in pure and sweet from the gulf; and even the pestilential fogs that settle in for days at a time in winter have a lovely aspect viewed from the height of Lions Gate Bridge.

It began as a lumber town in the 1860s, centred on a tavern kept by Gassy Jack Deighton. Lumber is still vital to Vancouver, but the old forests that stood here at the mouth of the Fraser River are gone, except for the remnant in Stanley Park. The logs (chiefly spruce and fir, plate 167) come down the coast (in Davis rafts) towed by tugboats to Vancouver's mills for pro-cessing into plywood, pulp, and lumber. Hollyburn Ridge (plate 167, background) rises above the down-town skyline, seen from False Creek in the centre of town. The British Columbia Power Commission Building, an example of the modern commercial architecture of the city, stands at right, behind the C.P.R. yards.

The city is too new to have a defined character yet, but there are signs of the way it must develop. The early tendency to variety, when the town was wide open to all kinds of people, shut off abruptly with the passing of discriminatory immigration laws. The laws were declared illegal by Ottawa; nevertheless they reduced the influx of East Indians, Japanese, and Chinese (plate 168, the old Chinatown on West Pender Street). Today, immigrants from Europe and eastern Canada, and a few from Asia, are slowly threading new colours into the Anglo-Saxon cloth. From a close concentration on money and politics, Vancouver has turned to a wary interest in 'useless' things. Its painters – Bobak, Smith, Binning – were among the best in Canada during a post-war surge of creative activity here, and its writers – Earle Birney, Eric Nicol, and the sad visitor, Malcolm Lowry – produced some of the most interesting writing in Canada in the fifties. Vancouver buildings have won national prizes (e.g. the Massey Gold Medal for architecture for Thea Koerner House at the University of British Columbia), and the new Massey College in Toronto was designed by a member of a Vancouver firm. The post-and-beam house, whose first thorough development in Canada was here, is prevalent in the suburbs (plate 170, overlooking Howe Sound, north of Vancouver). The post-and-beam house has been widely imitated in the rest of Canada. Sports – racing, football, swimming, rowing, golf, tennis – are all phenomenally popular, largely owing to the long season. The University of British Columbia, which is both big and very progressive in its attitudes, has outlived the time when Easterners condescended to its awkwardness, and is now recognized as one of the best universities in Canada.

When you look down to the end of a street in Vancouver, often you are staring into a green sea of leaves. This is not always a case of haphazard development into the surrounding rain forest, for Vancouver people have freckled their city with parks. The biggest, Stanley Park, has formidable crowds, trees, and zoo; the smaller ones, like Queen Elizabeth Park (plate 169), are simply refreshing. Queen Elizabeth Park is laid out in a pleasant rambling pattern on various levels and the paths connecting the gardens are left relatively wild.

In most parts of the city, there is a remarkable sense of not being in a city at all. When you stand on Georgia Street, down town, and can look up at Hollyburn, or Grouse Mountain (3,900 feet); when you drive home from work over Lions Gate Bridge to North or West Vancouver and look West over deep sea, the sense of release from pressure is blessed. Often on a warm day, office-workers take a sandwich lunch down to the shore at English Bay, an arc of sand built up by the Fraser. The river's yellow sands boil out into the gulf and are pushed back to shore by tide and wind, where they have built up English Bay and a whole peninsula of beaches round Point Grey. At Spanish Banks (plate 171) on this shore, great logs broken away from the log booms are washed up. People frequently come down to cut off a piece and chop it up for firewood. They run the risk of being caught by logging company officials, for the stamp driven into the end of the softwood logs compacts the fibres into the owner's brand ten feet or more down the length of the log.

The clouds that hang over Vancouver are familiar (plate 173, looking at the city from Lions Gate Bridge, Stanley Park, in front of the down-town area). The city is the dullest in Canada during the winter months, as well as the rainiest. The view reversed (plate 172) shows the Lions Gate Bridge from Vancouver Harbour.

174-6   Burrard Inlet, a long, narrow street of water lined on both sides with docks, begins just east of here (plate 174), between Point Atkinson (foreground) and Point Grey (upper left). The inlet is Vancouver's harbour, the dividing-line between residential North Vancouver and down town, and the obstacle between the city proper and the mainland to the north. Vancouver is Canada's second port in terms of total tonnage loaded and unloaded each year. Only Montreal handles more goods. By far the most important of the goods trans-shipped here is wheat, almost double the tonnage of the next bulkiest item, pulpwood and chips. The wheat comes down from the prairies by rail, and goes out from here to the trading world, including Red China and Russia.

The Gulf of Georgia (to the right) lies between the mainland and Vancouver Island, which is just visible through the mist (at upper centre and upper right). Over this gulf comes Vancouver's wet winter weather: the clouds gathered over the gulf, and the Pacific beyond, drive inland, blown by the prevailing westerlies. Lying on the edge of the Pacific, Victoria on Vancouver Island has a noticeably warmer, drier, and brighter winter, because of the influence of the relatively warm sea, which protects the whole southern tip of the island from cold polar air, and because its surrounding land is low. The warm, damp air from the Pacific can pass over Victoria at a low altitude, but it must rise to pass over the coast wall backing Vancouver; and there, cooled, it turns to fog or rain. Vancouver does not get a remarkable number of inches of rain (only fifty-four in the average year, plus two feet of snow), but what it does get is concentrated in winter and spread over a disheartening number of days (average: twenty-five in December, twenty-three in January, including snowy days). Still, there is a place on the island, called Henderson Lake, which makes this seem arid: at Henderson Lake were set several North American rain records – 323 inches in a year, and eighty inches in one month. The south end of Vancouver Island (twenty-five inches in an average year) is indisputably the pleasantest place in

Canada to live. The gardening season is virtually year-round; there have been winters with no frost at all; in most, there are fewer than twenty nights of it, even fewer days.

At Point No Point, near Victoria, on the Straits of Juan de Fuca, between the southern end of the island and the American mainland, the polished black rocks smoothed by tide and wave rise like whalebacks (plate 176). The tides here are relatively low, and the earth is covered with shore grasses (plate 175) almost to the edge of the water, even at low tide. You seldom see that long extent of tidal foreshore, wet, puddled, and stinking of the sea, so common in the east. Along the coast here, if there is such a low shore, it is often covered at low tide with abalone pickers wading out in hipboots to take the molluscs from the rocks.

These straits between the small Canadian off-shore islands and the American ones in the distance (plate 176, background, includes the Canadian islands nearest camera, with the Olympic Mountains of the United States in the far background) are the last of Canada for ships heading west. The ocean is in a lull here, but when the gales come, as they frequently do in winter, the coast disappears under the flying spray of waves fifty feet high. The worst storms are from the south-east (camera direction, due south). At such moments these summer-blown drift logs, probably broken loose from a raft far to the north, are picked up and thrown scores of feet inland.

In summer, the season when these photographs were taken, the shore is delightful. The swimming season is short (from June to early September) considering the mild winters. The reason is that it takes the ocean months to warm up. The air temperature, directly influenced by the ocean, rises at a rate which for Canada is remarkably slow in spring – less than ten degrees difference in the means of March and May. The change in fall is similar – less than twelve degrees difference between September and November. Given a warm day, you come after your swim at Point No Point up the hill to an English-style teahouse overlooking the ocean, where you can have wine with your dinner of fresh Coast salmon. Canada has come no closer to serenity than this.

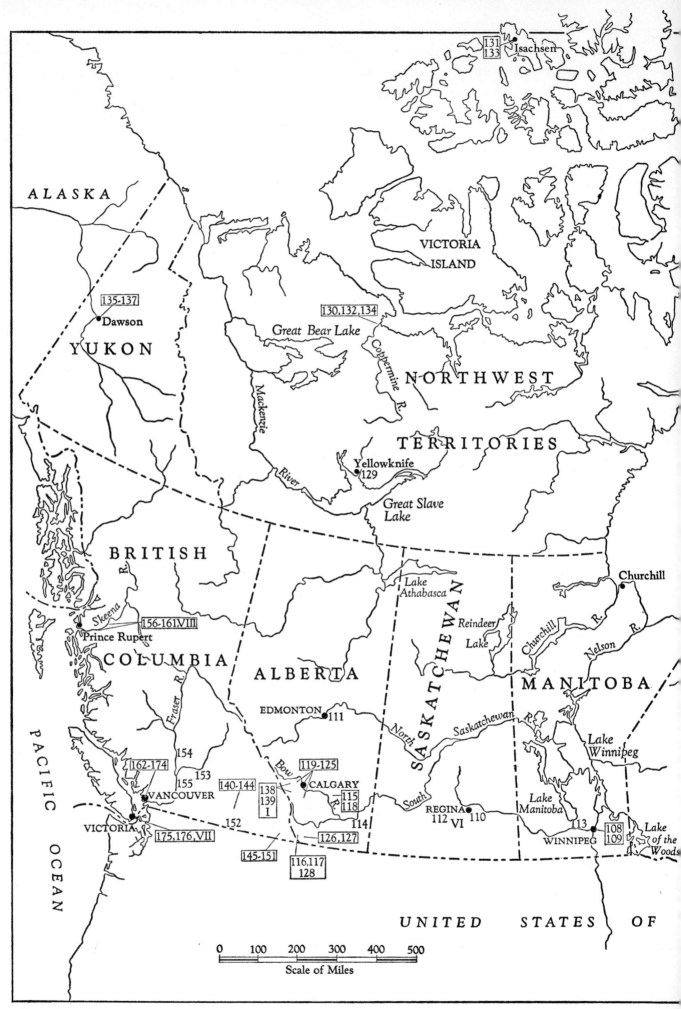

ALASKA

131
133 ·Isachsen

135-137
·Dawson

YUKON

VICTORIA
ISLAND

Great Bear Lake

130,132,134

NORTHWEST

Mackenzie

Coppermine R.

TERRITORIES

River

Yellowknife
·129

Great Slave
Lake

BRITISH

Lake
Athabasca

Churchill

Reindeer
Lake

Churchill R.

Nelson R.

COLUMBIA

Skeena R.

156-161,VIII

Prince Rupert

ALBERTA

SASKATCHEWAN

MANITOBA

North Saskatchewan R.

Saskatchewan R.

EDMONTON
·111

Lake
Winnipeg

PACIFIC

Fraser R.

154

155   153

162-174

VANCOUVER

140-144

Bow

138
139
I

119-125

CALGARY

115
118

Lake
Manitoba

South R.

REGINA
112   VI

110

113

Lake
of the
Woods

108
109

152

114

VICTORIA

175,176,VII

126,127

WINNIPEG

145-151

116,117
128

OCEAN

UNITED   STATES   OF

0   100   200   300   400   500

Scale of Miles

The numbers refer to plates. See also index of place names overleaf.

GREENLAND

BAFFIN BAY

BAFFIN ISLAND

HUDSON BAY

James Bay

QUEBEC

NEWFOUNDLAND

Davis Inlet
31,32

LABRADOR

30
North West
River
Hamilton

23-29,II

ST. JOHN'S

St. Lawrence R.
2, 4
1 5 3

PRINCE
EDWARD I.

ONTARIO

Lake
Nipigon

107 Marathon

Lake Superior

106

103,104

101
102

105

90-100

AMERICA

Lake Michigan

Lake Huron

TORONTO
80-85

L. Ontario

88,89

Lake Erie

WINDSOR

33-40

QUEBEC

41-43

SAINT JOHN

NEW
BRUNSWICK

6-8

NOVA
SCOTIA
22 HALIFAX
20,21,III

9-19 Lunenburg

47-58,IV

MONTREAL
61 46 44
       45

67-70

59

OTTAWA
60,73,V

62-66

76-78

71,72,74
75,79

86,87

ATLANTIC OCEAN

GM

INDEX OF LOCALITIES

Numbers in brackets are Introduction page numbers. All other numbers are plate numbers, italicized when referring to an illustration, roman type when referring to a mention in the notes on the plates.

THE PLATES

PLANCHES

1 LES MECHINS, Québec ▶

2 ST-YVON
Québec

3 GRANDE-VALLEE, Québec

4 ST-YVON, Québec

HARBOUR, MONT LOUIS, Quebec
LE HAVRE, MONT-LOUIS, Québec

6, 7, 8 FARMS NEAR SUSSEX, New Brunswick   FERMES PRES DE SUSSEX, Nouveau-Brunswick

10 DRAGGER NET, LUNENBURG
CHALUT, LUNENBURG

9 UNLOADING COD, LUNENBURG, Nova Scotia
DECHARGEMENT DE LA MORUE, LUNENBURG, Nouvelle-Ecosse

11 ADZING SHIP'S RIBS, LUNENBURG, Nova Scotia ● DOLAGE DE LA MEMBRURE D'UN BATEAU,
LUNENBURG, Nouvelle-Ecosse

12 DORIES, BLUE ROCKS, Nova Scotia
DORIS, BLUE ROCKS, Nouvelle-Ecosse

13 DRAGGER ● CHALUTIER, LUNENBURG

14 LUNENBURG HARBOUR, Nova Scotia ● PORT DE LUNENBURG, Nouvelle-Ecosse

15, 16, 17 TYPICAL FRAME HOUSES
TYPE COMMUN DE MAISONS EN BOIS, LUNENBURG

19 FAMILY BURIAL PLOT ● SEPULTURE FAMILIALE, LUNENBURG

18 ST JOHN'S CHURCH, LUNENBURG, Nova Scotia
L'EGLISE ST-JEAN, LUNENBURG, Nouvelle-Ecosse

20 MAHONE BAY, Nova Scotia ● Nouvelle-Ecosse ▶

21 TOWN OF MAHONE BAY, Nova Scotia ● VILLE DE MAHONE BAY, Nouvelle-Ecosse

22 HALIFAX HARBOUR, Nova Scotia ● HALIFAX: LE PORT, Nouvelle-Ecosse

23 UPPER BATTERY, ST JOHN'S, Newfoundland ● LA BATTERIE HAUTE, ST-JEAN, Terre-Neuve

24, 25 ST JOHN'S ● ST·JEAN

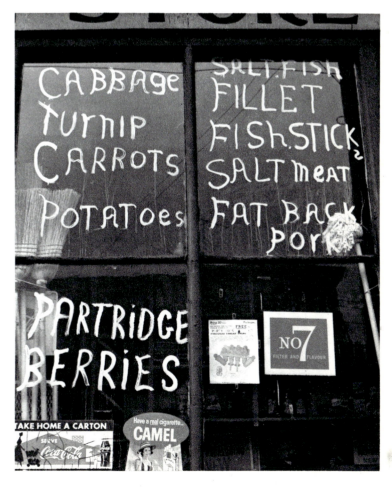

27 CABOT TOWER, ST JOHN'S ● LA TOUR DE CABOT, ST-JEAN

26 SUGAR LOAF HEAD, ST JOHN'S, Newfoundland
LE PAIN-DE-SUCRE, ST-JEAN, Terre-Neuve

28 BATTERIES FROM SIGNAL HILL, ST JOHN'S, Newfoundland ● LES BATTERIES VUES DE LA COL-
LINE DU SIGNAL, ST-JEAN, Terre-Neuve

29   ST   JOHN'S

ARBOUR ● LE PORT DE ST-JEAN

30 NASKAPI INDIANS ● INDIENS NASKAPI, NORTH WEST RIVER, Labrador

32 WIGWAM, DAVIS INLET, Labrador

31 DAVIS INLET, Labrador

33 HARBOUR, QUEBEC CITY • QUEBEC: LE PORT

34 CHATEAU FRONTENAC, FROM COTE DE LA MONTAGNE ● LE CHATEAU FRONTENAC VU
DE LA COTE DE LA MONTAGNE, QUEBEC

35 LOWER TOWN, CHAMPLAIN STREET ● RUE CHAMPLAIN, BASSE-VILLE, QUEBEC

36 ST LOUIS STREET ● RUE ST-LOUIS, QUEBEC

37 NOTRE-DAME-DE-QUEBEC, QUEBEC

38 RUE DE LA FABRIQUE, UPPER TOWN • HAUTE-VILLE
QUEBEC

39 ST FLAVIEN STREET • RUE ST-FLAVIEN, QUEBEC

40 CITADEL AND BOARDWALK

FROM THE CHATEAU ● LA CITADELLE ET LA PROMENADE DE LA TERRACE VUES DU CHATEAU, QUEBEC

41 FENCES, ST MICHEL, Quebec ● CLOTURES, ST/MICHEL, Québec

42, 43 FARMS NEAR ST MICHEL
FERMES PRES DE ST-MICHEL

44 LAKE MASSAWIPPI, EASTERN TOWNSHIPS, ● LAC MASSAWIPPI, CANTONS DE L'EST, ▶

45 MAPLE WOODS, EASTERN TOWNSHIPS, Quebec
ERABLIERS, CANTONS DE L'EST, Québec

46 COUNTRY CHURCH, EASTERN TOWNSHIPS
EGLISE RURALE, CANTONS DE L'EST

47, 48
CHARITY AND
COMMERCE

LA CHARITE
ET
LE COMMERCE

PLACE VILLE
MARIE,
MONTREAL,
Quebec

49 PLACE VILLE MARIE FROM METCALFE STREET ● PLACE VILLE-MARIE VUE DE LA RUE METCALFE, MONTREAL, Quebec

ENTRANCE TO VILLE MARIE FROM WEST ● PLACE VILLE-MARIE: FAÇADE OUEST, MONTREAL

52 PEEL AT ST
CATHERINE
RUE PEEL, COIN
STE-CATHERINE
MONTREAL

51
METCALFE AT
DORCHESTER
RUE METCALFE,
COIN DORCHESTER
MONTREAL, Quebec

53
BEAVER HALL HILL
COTE DU BEAVER
HALL
MONTREAL

54 LAFONTAINE PARK ● PARC LAFONTAINE, MONTREAL, Quebec

55 CATHEDRAL OF MARY QUEEN OF THE WORLD
CATHEDRALE MARIE-REINE-DU-MONDE, MONTREAL

56 ST LAMBERT LOCK • ECLUSE DE ST-LAMBERT, MONTREAL, Quebec

57 SHIPPING GRAIN,

MONTREAL   HARBOUR ● CHARGEMENT DU GRAIN, PORT DE MONTREAL

58 MONTREAL FROM ST HELEN'S ISLAND ● MONTREAL: LA CITE VUE DE L'ILE STE-HELENE, Quebec ▶

59 FLOODED AREAS, ST LAWRENCE SEAWAY, Quebec
TERRAINS INONDES, VOIE MARITIME DU SAINT-LAURENT, Québec

60 BOATHOUSE, RIDEAU CANAL
HANGAR A BATEAUX, CANAL RIDEAU, Ontario

61 LACHINE RAPIDS, ST

AWRENCE SEAWAY ● RAPIDES DE LACHINE, VOIE MARITIME DU SAINT-LAURENT

62 INTERNATIONAL BRIDGE • PONT INTERNATIONAL, CORNWALL   63 PAPER MILL REFLECTION • REFLET

D'UNE PAPETERIE, CORNWALL, Ontario

64 FRENCH/ROBERTSON HOUSE, UPPER CANADA VILLAGE ● LA MAISON FRENCH/ROBERTSON, VILLAGE DU HAUT-CANADA, Ontario

65 LOUCKS HOUSE, UPPER CANADA VILLAGE
LA MAISON LOUCKS, VILLAGE DU HAUT-CANADA

66 HIRED MAN'S HOUSE, UPPER CANADA VILLAGE
LA MAISON DE L'ENGAGE, VILLAGE DU HAUT-CANADA, Ontario ▶

67 PARLIAMENT BUILDINGS
EDIFICES DU PARLEMENT, OTTAWA, Ontario

68 WEST BLOCK, PARLIAMENT BUILDINGS
L'EDIFICE PARLEMENTAIRE DE L'OUEST, OTTAWA

71 AUTUMN FIELD ● UN CHAMP A L'AUTOMNE, GANANOQUE, Ontario

72 VINE AND ROCK ● VIGNE ET ROC, Ontario

73 MAPLE WOOD ● UNE ERABLIERE, Ontario

74 SUMAC, Ontario

75 NEAR LANSDOWNE ● PRES DE LANSDOWNE, Ontario

77 CITY HALL
HOTEL DE VILLE
BROCKVILLE

76 VICTORIAN HOUSE
MAISON DE
STYLE VICTORIEN
BROCKVILLE, Ontario

78 STONE CHURCH
EGLISE DE PIERRE
BROCKVILLE

79 ROYAL MILITARY
COLLEGE
COLLEGE MILITAIRE
ROYAL
KINGSTON, Ontario ▶

81 NATIONAL BALLET REHEARSAL ● LE BALLET NATIONAL EN REPETITION, TORONTO, Ontario

◀ 80 WATERFRONT, TORONTO
TORONTO: LA CITE VUE DE LA BAIE

2 ST LAWRENCE
MARKET
LE MARCHE ST-
LAURENT
TORONTO

83 SKYLINE FROM PARK PLAZA HOTEL ● LA CITÉ VUE DE L'HOTEL PARK PLAZA, TORONTO, Ontario

84 BLOOR STREET
LA RUE BLOOR
TORONTO

85 TORONTO ISLAND ● LES ILES DE TORONTO, Ontario

86 HORSESHOE FALLS ● LA CHUTE EN FER A CHEVAL, NIAGARA FALLS, Ontario

87 HORSESHOE FALLS FROM SEAGRAM TOWER
LA CHUTE EN FER A CHEVAL VUE DE LA TOUR SEAGRAM ▶

88, 89 'TROILUS AND CRESSIDA' ● 'TROILUS ET CRESSIDA', STRATFORD, Ontario

90 CALEDON HILLS, NEAR ALTON ● LES COLLINES DE CALEDON, PRES D'ALTON, Ontario

92 HARVESTING OATS ● MOISSON DE L'AVOINE,
COLLINGWOOD, Ontario

93 COLLINGWOOD HILLS ● LES COLLINES DE COLLINGWOOD

91 HOCKLEY VALLEY ● LA VALLEE HOCKLEY, Ontario

94 COLLINGWOOD HILLS • LES COLLINES DE COLLINGWOOD, Ontario

95 ALBION HILLS ● LES COLLINES ALBION, Ontario

96 DUNDALK PLATEAU ● LE PLATEAU DE DUNDALK, Ontario

97 HARDWOOD BUSH IN MARCH ● BOIS FRANCS EN MARS, Ontario

98 APPLE ORCHARD ● VERGER DE POMMIERS, COLLINGWOOD, Ontario

99 DEVIL'S GLEN ● LE VALLON DU DIABLE, COLLINGWOOD ▶

100 ICE SHOVE • POUSSEE DE BLOCS DE GLACE CONTRE LA RIVE, THORNBURY, Ontario

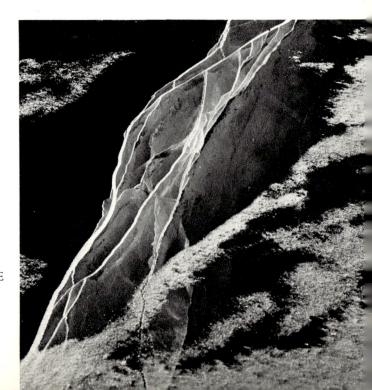

101 ICE CRACK • FISSURE DANS LA GLACE

102 SHAWANAGA, GEORGIAN BAY ● BAIE GEORGIENNE, Ontario

103 GRANITE AND PINE, MANITOULIN ISLAND
GRANIT ET PIN, ILE MANITOULIN, Ontario

104 SQUARED LOG BARN, MANITOULIN ISLAND
GRANGE BATIE DE TRONCS EQUARRIS, ILE MANITOULIN

105 BRUCE PENINSULA
PENINSULE DE BRUCE, Ontario

106 LAKE SUPERIOR PROVINCIAL PARK
PARC PROVINCIAL DU LAC SUPERIEUR, Ontario

107 MARATHON, LAKE SUPERIOR
MARATHON, LAC SUPERIEUR

108, 109 WINNIPEG, Manitoba

111 EDMONTON, Alberta

110 REGINA, Saskatchewan

112 SOUTHERN PRAIRIE, NEAR MOOSE JAW ▶

SECTEUR SUD DES PRAIRIES, PRES DE
MOOSE JAW, Saskatchewan

113 C.P.R. TRACK CREW ● EQUIPE D'ENTRETIEN DES VOIES DU C.P.R., Manitoba

114 C.P.R. TRANSCONTINENTAL LINE ● VOIE TRANSCONTINENTALE DU C.P.R., Alberta

115 BADLANDS, DINOSAUR VALLEY ● PHENOMENES D'EROSION, VALLEE DU DINOSAURE, Alberta ▶

116 ALDER BLUFF ● TOUFFE D'AUNES, WILLOW VALLEY, Alberta

117 ALDER LEAF ● FEUILLE D'AUNE, Alberta

118 DESERT CACTUS, Southern Alberta
CACTUS DES TERRES ARIDES, Sud de l'Alberta

120 STONY INDIAN RESERVATION • LA RESERVE INDIENNE STONY, Alberta

◀ 119 CALGARY, Alberta

121 GRAIN ELEVATORS • ELEVATEURS A GRAINS, HIGH RIVER, Alberta

123 HIGHWOOD RIVER ● RIVIERE HIGHWOOD, Alberta

122 RANCHER AND SON, HIGHWOOD VALLEY, Alberta
PROPRIETAIRE D'UN RANCH ET SON FILS, HIGHWOOD VALLEY, Alberta

124 RANGELAND, FOOTHILLS • PATURAGES, COLLINES DE PIEDMONT, Alberta

125 PIEBALD HORSES • CHEVAUX PIE, Alberta

126 PINCHER CREEK, Alberta

127 APPROACHING CROW'S NEST PASS ● AUX ABORDS DE LA PASSE DU NID DE CORBEAU, Alberta

128 WILLOW VALLEY, Alberta ▶

129 YELLOWKNIFE, Northwest Territories
YELLOWKNIFE, Territoires du Nord-ouest

130 COPPERMINE RIVER, Northwest Territories
COPPERMINE RIVER, Territoires du Nord-ouest

131 ISACHSEN, ELLEF RINGNES ISLAND, 79°N, Northwest Territories
ISACHSEN, ILE ELLEF RINGNES, 79°N, Territoires du Nord-ouest

132 COPPERMINE RIVER, Northwest Territories ● Territoires du Nord-ouest

133 ISACHSEN, Northwest Territories ● Territoires du Nord-ouest

134 COPPERMINE RIVER

135 MOOSEHIDE, DAWSON CITY, Yukon

136 BLACK MIKE WINAGE

137 DAWSON CITY

138 KANANASKIS RIVER ● RIVIERE KANANASKIS, Alberta

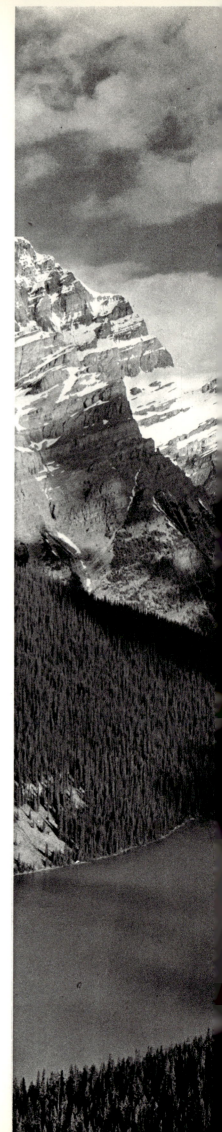

139 PEYTO LAKE ● LAC PEYTO, Alberta

140 GLACIER NATIONAL PARK
British Columbia
PARC NATIONAL DU GLACIER
Colombie Britannique

142 (opposite page) HERMIT RANGE, SELKIRK MOUNTAINS
CHAINE DE L'ERMITE, MONTS SELKIRK

141 C.P.R. BRIDGE, MOUNT TUPPER ● PONT DU C.P.R., MONT TUPPER

◀ 144 DAIRY FARM ● FERME LAITIERE, REVELSTOKE

145, 146 RANGE LAND, CRANBROOK, British Columbia
PATURAGES, CRANBROOK, Colombie Britannique

147 CHURCH, FORT STEELE • EGLISE, FORT STEELE

148, 149, 150 KOOTENAY LAKE, British Columbia
LAC KOOTENAY, Colombie Britannique

152 DRY-BELT FARM • FERME DE LA ZONE ARIDE, GRAND FORKS

151 NELSON FERRY, KOOTENAY LAKE, British Columbia
NELSON: LE TRAVERSIER, LAC KOOTENAY, Colombie Britannique

153 THOMPSON RIVER IN THE DRY BELT, British Columbia
LA RIVIERE THOMPSON DANS LA ZONE ARIDE, Colombie Britannique

154 FRASER RIVER NEAR LILLOOET • LE FLEUVE FRASER PRES DE LILLOOET

155 FRASER CANYON • LE CANYON DU FRASER

156 SKEENA RIVER, British Columbia ● LE FLEUVE SKEENA, Colombie Britannique

157 FARM NEAR KITWANGA • FERME PRES DE KITWANGA

158 MT CATT, SKEENA VALLEY • LE MONT CATT, VALLEE DU SKEENA

159 BURIAL HOUSE, KITWANCOOL, British Columbia ● SEPULTURE, KITWANCOOL, Colombie Britannique

160 TOTEMS,
KITWANCOOL

161 BURIAL HOUSE ● SEPULTURE, KITWANCOOL

163-165 RAIN FOREST DETAILS ● DETAILS CARACTERISTIQUES DE LA FORET EN ZONE HUMIDE

166 TOTEM, VANCOUVER

168 CHINATOWN ● LE QUARTIER CHINOIS, VANCOUVER

167 VANCOUVER FROM FALSE CREEK, British Columbia
VANCOUVER: LA CITE VUE DE FALSE CREEK, Colombie Britannique

169 QUEEN ELIZABETH PARK • LE PARC REINE ELIZABETH, VANCOUVER

170 RESIDENCE, HOWE

171 SPANISH BANKS
LES BANCS ESPAGNOLS
VANCOUVER

172, 173 VANCOUVER HARBOUR

ANCOUVER: LE PORT

175 VANCOUVER ISLAND ● L'ILE DE VANCOUVER

174 GULF OF GEORGIA, British Columbia

LE GOLFE DE GEORGIE, Colombie Britannique

176 STRAITS OF JUAN DE FUCA, British Columbia
LE DETROIT DE JUAN DE FUCA, Colombie Britannique